ONE GOOD OUTFIT

ONE GOOD OUTFIT

Jocelyn Brown

THE MERCURY PRESS

The publisher gratefully acknowledges the financial assistance of the Canada Council for the Arts and the Ontario Arts Council. The publisher further acknowledges the financial support of the Government of Canada through the Department of Canadian Heritage's Book Publishing Industry Development Program (BPIDP) for our publishing activities.

Edited by Beverley Daurio
Composition and page design by TASK
Printed and bound in Canada
Printed on acid-free paper

1 2 3 4 5 04 03 02 01 00

Canadian Cataloguing in Publication Data

Brown, Jocelyn, 1957–
One good outfit

ISBN 1-55128-080-9
1. Canadian wit and humour (English).★ I. Title.
PS8553.R68724O53 2000   C818'.602   C00-932198-5
PR9199.3.B6985.O53 2000

The Mercury Press
www.themercurypress.com

For
Anita, Claire, David,
Elizabeth, Marney, and Judy
with much love.

one
robe
many paths

— Ch'ung L'ing

Nothing but sandy soil and lots of rocks

Thirsty throat sore

War

then wore

One   good out

fit for

more

yet more   till

All is One

seamless soft and not undone

— bixter

PREFACE

When the human journey is finally over, the continuous presence of one good outfitters will surely be recalled. For we have been at every fork in the road, appropriately dressed and pleasant. From the Last Supper with Jesus to the Dinner Party with Judy, from oysters and Guinness in Clarinbridge to babaganoush in Tel Aviv, we were there. Inconspicuously, harmoniously there. Expert travelers, we carried no maps and left faint tracks.

Until now, that is. As the oracles of Fym Gwair foretold, the age of one good outfitting is upon us. We must prepare: countless novices need direction, and we veterans are not great enough in number to provide adequate counsel. During last year's convocation season, when three novices were ejected from graduation banquets in this city alone, the urgent need for a guidebook was painfully clear. And so, the world's first explicit manual on one good outfitting was authored by Evelyn of Edmonton. What an excellent product it is. Within these pages, the novice one good outfitter will find her mentor: she will be advised, soothed, educated and congratulated. She will find practical tips on securing shoes, alongside metaphysical training; she will learn how to enter a room and how to take its energetic reading. Most importantly, perhaps, the novice will discover her ancestors.

As I reread Evelyn's lucid historical accounts, I cannot help but wonder what the Sisters of the Cloth or the Prague group would think. Would they be amazed at our numbers? Perhaps not. As early as the twelfth century, Alisonne St. James prophesied "that the womynne of one gudd outfytt wyll flurish cross the lande and they wyll et well." Would they be impressed by our ingenuity? I hope so. But then, who could have been more ingenious than Frances Moret Rean in the court of Charles II or Sister Elizabeth in eighteenth century Provence? They would, I am certain, approve of Evelyn's work with gusto. At some magnificent celestial feast they are flipping these pages in delight. Finally, they have been given homage, and finally, they can see where their brave explorations have led. We have arrived.

Gerry Masooka

PART I: ONE GOOD OUTFIT

One good outfit

An explanation

The essential nature of my one good outfit is hard to pin down— it is not a dress, a blazer, a good pair of shoes, nor is it the collection of all these parts. Yet it exists. If you were sitting beside me you could feel the nap of the wool blazer, admire the piping around the neckline of the black shift underneath it, and if you were observant, you would notice that the shoes are *Avanti* because I have crossed my legs to the side in such a way that the big *A* on the soles is visible. You might say to yourself, *What a smartly dressed woman,* or *How elegant.* More to the point, you would not say to me, *What are you doing here?*

We might shift our focus, then, from the material of my outfit to its function. My one good outfit lets me fit into places that otherwise would be off limits. It is my passport to conferences, conventions, galas, art openings, and many other types of events where quality food is served. For eight years now, I have dined in style at every kind of gathering imaginable without having a penny to my name.

Of course, my outfit is not useful without me. It can't get far on its own and it might hang like a sack on someone else.

When I wear my outfit, people do not distinguish it from who I am. Other participants at, let's say, a political convention don't think, *What a nice outfit; I wonder if the woman wearing it should be here?* From their perspective my one good outfit is not about form or function— it is my state of being. But, am I not more than my outfit? I do not stop existing once I've taken it off. So it cannot be me.

We could go on and on, forever unfolding the meaning of my one good outfit, but we would never find it. Instead let us understand that it is many things, but no one thing. It has substance but is far more than fabric; it serves a purpose but cannot function alone; it makes a person, but the person remains when it is removed. I cannot say to you that my one good outfit is exactly this or that, only that it is all these things to me. And so I cannot say your one good outfit must be exactly so. I can only tell you what I know about having one good outfit and using it, and because every day is completely different, there is no straightforward way to do this. You must put together the pieces for yourself. Then you must draw your own conclusions, and proceed with your own tastes and intentions.

In the beginning

An inventory

It is helpful to start with a lifetime wardrobe inventory. The first clothing to empower me was the green plaid jumper and white shirt Aunt Mel gave me in grade four. For two years I wore it to every exam... and I always felt right (although my marks varied widely). It was my first one good outfit. There was a mauve pantsuit in grade eight, with stretchy bell-bottoms and contrasting white pompoms around the neckline of the stretchy top. And in grade ten, my last year of school, there was the orange minidress and chain belt that allowed me to go into the King Edward Hotel for coffee, and the Evergreen Lounge for Singapore slings, when my classmates could not. I can also remember my sister's one good outfits and my best friend Linda's. It is sometimes easier to see the effects of another person's one good outfit than your own. My sister Rita would transform from a big lump with hair in her eyes to an elegant woman who would be welcome anywhere. She wore wide-legged black pants— we called them "palazzos" then— with a bolero jacket trimmed in red soutache.

Taking stock

As you recall good outfits from your past, take note of common characteristics, even though the styles and probably the sizes varied. My sister, being tall and gaunt, always favoured generously cut, billowy things in black with striking trims and accessories in contrasting colours. Being on the more substantial side, I preferred classic cuts, and except for the green plaid jumper, monochromatic colour schemes. After sketching four one good outfits from my past, I drew up the following list of design features that remained constant:

> bias-bound necklines
> tab closures
> piping
> single welt pockets
> innovative plackets
> unrestricted waistlines
> stable fabrics

If you don't sketch, and must rely entirely on memory, use this checklist to help recall details:

> colour
> texture
> weight

ornamentation
proximity to body (fitted or loose)

If you can't remember one good outfit in your past, simply imagine what you would have liked to wear, think about what you'd like to have on now, and use the same checklist. As Virginia Woolf once said, *Memory is a capricious seamstress,* and to be honest, my mauve pantsuit may have been Rita's. The idea here is to identify a personal style, not get bogged down in historical data.

Current trends

Keeping in mind that we are still considering only the appearance of one good outfit, which is far from all of it, we will take the next step in determining your one good outfit and consult the experts. Perhaps you followed the UNO (United in Non-attachment and Oneness) design competitions last Fall, and saw coverage of the New York, Paris and Milan finals. Produced by Buddhist fashion designers, UNO requires competitors to design one outfit for life using CATE. A screening tool remarkably consistent with my own criteria for one good outfit selection, CATE stands for Compatible with the wearer; Adaptable to a changing environment; Timeless (good for at least two years); and Easy to care for. Here are sketches of the winning UNO designs:

  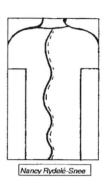

House of Rytt — Ying — *Nancy Rydelé-Snee*

UNO winning designs, 1997

Simple lines and synthetic fabrics clearly predominate, but note that each design has a distinctive feature— a double row of topstitching down the center, a large leather button, or a Guatemalan scarf.

Conceptualizing

Consider the UNO designs, review your checklist of personal preferences, and take the time you need to sketch or imagine your ideal one good outfit. Apply CATE to it and make whatever adjustments are necessary. Try to be clear about what's essential to you: if everything you've ever liked to wear has had long two-piece sleeves, then that is what you must have. On the other hand, don't get stuck on too many details unless you have the resources and talent to actually create something yourself. The ideal you are now formulating is only a reference point— a place to begin your one good outfit search.

(NB: From this point on, the abbreviations *ogoer, ogoers* and *ogo* will be used respectively for "one good outfitter," "one good outfitters," and "one good outfit.")

Components

Dress

It took four days and many miles to assemble my current one good outfit. I started at St. Vincent de Paul. It is the only used clothing depot for Catholics, so all good Catholic clothes are concentrated there, whereas decent Protestant garments are spread throughout dozens of Salvation Army and Goodwill stores. I found my dress in the dollar bin, wrinkled and getting on in years, but obviously of fine quality. I was taken with the clean, fluid lines of its princess seams, and the luxurious texture of its fabric— a type of black linen no longer available in the West. Although a shorter hem was required, the styling was becoming on me, especially the simple neckline— which is edged in quarter-inch piping, as mentioned. The short sleeves add to its daywear versatility but detract slightly from its ability to be chic at cocktail parties and art openings.

Jacket

I went to three Goodwill stores and an estate sale before coming upon my blazer at a consignment store. Generally, consignment stores are well beyond my means, but at this one I discovered the back room where things are sorted. I saw the blazer on a rack immediately, unpriced and unpressed, and simply exchanged it for the kangaroo jacket I was wearing, which had many more years of wear in it. The camel colour was not part of my ideal one good outfit, but this blazer has proven itself wonderfully, being warm and versatile. Single-breasted, in a summerweight Italian wool, it has three black leather buttons which pick up the dress beautifully, and at hip length is perfect for my body type.

Jacket label

A good jacket label is important as it can be displayed when the jacket is removed and draped over a chair or one's arm. With luck you may find a nice Ports blazer at your favourite thrift store, but chances are you will have to get the jacket one place and the label another. I wore my grey jacket and dress to Holts, where I took many suits into the fitting room. Rachel, sales associate, was insistent with her how-are-you-doing-in-there's so I had to be quick with the razor blade. (Fortunately I was in a dressing room with a proper door that could be locked— do avoid curtained change rooms, as sales people silently appear without warning, especially during end-of-season sales, when the public flocks in.) There are other, less stressful, ways to get labels, but these depend on serendipity. Some of you may know of Marnie Treckle's label bonanza at the Fascioniste Show in Montreal last year, where, backstage, she discovered an entire roll of Puzz labels. (In Halifax, Faith's intrepid sister Hannah used her social and media connections to promote Puzz, thereby making the label useful to Maritime *ogoers*.) Raging anti-bourgeois designers may simply give you their labels. NAKIT, for example, has been very generous to Mimsy Burroughs and other Manchester-area *ogoers*.

Calvin Klein, DKNY and Donna Karan labels are good because they aren't sewn all the way around, just tacked at the corners. You will need to remember this when sewing one in.

Experts stress the importance of jackets. There are now several fashion books devoted only to jacket selection, and even the most general clothing guides claim that a jacket is key to any wardrobe's success. Perhaps you're familiar with Lady Sarah Hawkins, who wrote in her famous *Notes to a Daughter*, "A good jacket will advance you further than any degree, pedigree or spouse." For ongoing guidance on this essential item consult the *Jacket Jill* column in *DressMe*, which last month, for example, advised, "Shawl collars make one's neck appear longer."

Shoes

For shoes, visit Buddhist meditation centres in your city and yoga-type places, where people go to practise non-attachment, usually in bare feet with their eyes closed. Many of them own very good shoes. This is how I found mine, black pumps with a stacked heel and smart covered buckle. Good shoes can also be found in authentic Japanese restaurants, where they will be carefully placed outside of enclosed eating areas. In the fall, between sandal and boot seasons, many pairs of new shoes are lined up in porches where house parties are underway. Try to get invited to a big Thanksgiving get-together. Do remember that non-Buddhists are attached to their belongings and will be dismayed to lose their shoes. Leave something in return, if only a note of thanks.

Hosiery

For those of us who go the dress route, opaque tights go with short hemlines, pantyhose for anything below the knee (as stipulated in *Hose by any Other Name*). Pants people need plain black socks, or black socks with little grey diamonds on them. Unless you're wearing a lab coat for a medical specialization, never ever wear white socks or hose.

Hosiery products can be easily found in change rooms at swimming pools and fitness centres. Tell the cashier, *I forgot my bathing suit* without coming to a full stop, and she'll let you through. Check the Lost and Found box, which is usually in a cupboard under the sinks, although a few places keep it behind the front desk. The downtown YMCA in Edmonton has a good Lost and Found in its corporate change room (not in the public one), but the best L&F's are in private fitness clubs. Phone ahead for a free introductory class and tour, enjoy a nice sauna and shower, and see what you can find. Friday after lunch is the best time as things have accumulated over the week. A private fitness club is especially cordial if you indicate a corporate connection and ask about group rates. I introduce myself as the EA (for executive assistant; always use the acronym) of the Japanese Business Association.

Accessories

According to at least one fashion expert, "The unaccessorized life is not worth living." Although not so extreme, certain *ogoers* think along these lines, and insist that every good outfit should begin with an outstanding belt or scarf. In the words of Maive Sullivan, who I consulted on this matter, "Once I found that bracelet, the rest of the outfit came running, honest to goodness, just appeared, a skirt here, a blazer there, and before you know it I had a winning team." To traditional thinkers like myself, this seems like building a house around a nice flower box, but Maive and I do concur that the flower box is an essential design feature.

Think access and you will understand the importance of accessories. I previously described one good outfit as a passport to the world of gourmet food. Now it is time to consider accessories as the visas to particular events. It is the right scarf, tied in the right way, that helps an *ogoer* to pass through hotel security into, for example, a public administrators' colloquium and brunch. And once inside, it will be a briefcase, pager or simple clipboard that assures fellow visitors you belong.

Sadly, some *ogoers* think "excessorize," especially, it seems, in the east, where a distaste for the open "a" sound has perhaps made this mistake inevitable. To excessorize is to terribly overdo one's accessories. When someone lumbers into an event with a massive daytimer, a pager strapped to her belt, a laptop slung over a shoulder, and jewellery glittering from ears, neck, and wrists, people say things like, *What's she trying to prove? Get real*, or, as I overheard at the family therapy awards dinner last week, *She doth project too much.*

Accessories fall into two major groups: group one is decorative (i.e., scarves, jewellery, hats) and group two is functional (i.e., pagers, laptops, whistles). I found my first group-two item: a clipboard with pages of checklists and a pen attached by a grubby beige string, in the Holiday Inn loading zone. It continues to be useful at complex theme events where music, food, waiters, and decorations must all be coordinated. Someone with a checklist fits right in, and although there will also be at least one "real" checklist person, there is plenty of checking for everyone at these things, and awkward confrontations are easily enough avoided. In 1989, at the opening night of *Isadora*, I came across my first group-one item in the green room. It was a silk organza scarf, dark green shot with sapphire blue, long enough to wrap as a belt, but light and flowy around the neck.

Next to jackets, scarves have inspired more fashion literature than any other wearable. Certainly the most radical of these texts is *Tying the Knot*, a guide to using one scarf as the only garment through life, by knotting it into a dress, sarong, bathing suit, pants and, finally, shroud. For the moderates among us, scarves are typically used as:

1) head wraps
2) neckpieces
3) arm slings
4) shawls, including the one-shoulder Scottish warrior
look, which also requires
5) a belt

For guidance on colour selection, see "knockout neutrals," "prints for pizazz," or "brash brights" in *Sensational Scarves* by Carol Strallij.

Cross-functional coordinates

The *ogoer* optimizes the performance of each part of her outfit by what is commonly known as mixing and matching. With basic components— dress, jacket, shoes, two accessories— I can create multiple looks to suit different types of functions. For instance, when I have to be both purposeful and sociable, say at a benefit, I wear everything, alternately checking things on my clipboard as I survey the room, then smoothing my scarf as I mingle. At the other extreme, when I have to flaunt indifference (medical conferences) or look edgy and spare (film shoots) I wear only the dress and shoes, sometimes attaching a bit of lint or food onto the dress. For high-security events I wear my dress and scarf and, carrying the clipboard, "pop in" to make sure everything is okay. Within earshot of a security person, I apologize to someone for only being able to stay for a few minutes, just long enough to check the buffet. My jacket is also left behind for weddings and funerals. A clean look is appreciated at both and I rely on my dress and scarf, draping the scarf for weddings and winding it around my neck for funerals.

The idea here is that every piece of your *ogo* can say many things, depending on what it is combined with and what context it is seen in. Try to see each item with fresh eyes rather than set ideas on what it can and cannot mix with. Combine pieces with abandon until each enjoys and happily complements the other. The more your *ogo* can reconfigure, the more liberty it will give you in return.

Decorative Accessories

High performance jewellery

Jewellery will say more about you than any other part of your *ogo*, and it's best to control the message carefully. One piece of jewellery is a badge of authenticity and self worth. A good piece of jewellery is a badge of authenticity (think of the queen's crown and the pope's ring). Fortunately for us, authenticity now means ephemeral and self-consiously fake, qualities most emphatically expressed with hand-made items. The best jewellery, in fact, is meta-fake, thanks to Coco Chanel, who used fake pearls to say, *I'm real*, although in her case the term was *faux*. Meta-fake items gleefully exaggerate their non-worth. Perhaps you know the "Great Unwatched" line of carboard timepieces (created by Anna Guin of Nelson) or Ellie T.'s styrofoam lorgnettes. "Found objects," especially rubbish, are ideal material for today's jewellery, especially when you can create ironic contrasts (i.e., domesticity versus the sacred; urban decay versus the sacred; technolology versus the sacred). My fusili ying/yang pin continues to be versatile, and I know Maddy Knight still gets good wear from her rubber tubing celtic cross. Consider attending one of Maddy's quarterly design studios if you live in

our area. In the fall session we set synthetic pearls into clustered
butts of foreign cigarettes.

Leather

Phone the bus depot and say you lost a very simple pair of lined
black leather gloves, you can't remember the label. They will
almost certainly have them for you.

Purses are a bother at most events, and completely wrong
at others, but a briefcase can be useful. It need not be leather.
For the potentially athletic among us, sporty bags with flaps and
pockets are the thing, as they suggest independent interests,
which are currently admirable. These bags are often slung over
chairs or plunked on the floor to further express sportiness, and
during coffee breaks one might find something appropriate
while bag owners caffeinate and chat. For a larger briefcase, the
tour bus boarding zones outside good hotels offer the best
opportunities. Lorraine Semnil, the performance poet/leather
specialist has written an entertaining series on obtaining luggage.
Intended for vocal performance, it is difficult to read, but for a
little change of pace here is an excerpt:

let go luggage let go		*Remember something.*
Big hotel. Tour Bus.		*Something big.*
Lonng Rows of		*Stride. (verb) To*
1) luggage 2) People		*Pick best brown one*
Mix (verb) with people		*Walk past group &*
Remark about day,	*hope it changes, hope it stays (choose one).*	*snap cell phone open.*

Briefcase contents

Never stuff a briefcase. It must be solid, but gaunt. When placed on a floor or table, it should make a clear, definite sound, like a large book being shut, and when you open it to get your daytimer or reading glasses, the following items should be evident: keys, coatcheck tag, hotel stationery and pen, airline peanuts, children's pictures, cup, computer disks, daytimer, and a small bottle of Chinese herbs.

Functional accessories

The nametag

A nametag ensures smooth, direct access. All nametags these days are hang-around-your-neck models. (In the late eighties when silk knits were popular, pin-on nametags caused a number of snags and consequent lawsuits.) Neck nametags have clear plastic covers with paper inserts that display a person's name and often the event logo. Some hotels, such as the Westin in my centre, provide nametag recycling boxes somewhere close to the exit. These are handy once an event is well underway and a few people have already left. Help yourself to a discarded nametag, remove the insert, write your name on the back of it in black felt pen and re-insert. At every event there are last minute registrants with handwritten nametags, so you will not be in the least conspicuous.

If you are attending a function from the beginning, get there early when the registration table is swamped by perfectionists wanting to make sure of this or that, and pluck a nametag off the table with a sure hand and understanding smile. Then reverse the insert as described above. Alternatively, you could wear whoever's name is on the right side of the tag, depending on the size of the conference, how well people seem to know each other, and the uniqueness of the name. This is risky, though, as I found out with Mary Johnson's tag at the LaLeche League's national conference in October. Although I had not heard of her, or *Duct Tapes*, her musical tribute to breast-feeding, other attendees certainly had and freely expressed their disappointment that I was not "the" Mary Johnson. I took the nametag off and put it in my pocket so it was visible but not readable.

Leona is pilot-testing a permanent nametag, made by Trudy from recycled rubber and brass. Fortunately Pat at *Keys Please* does engraving and feels beholden to Leona for reasons we need not get into. Worn while one also uses one's own coffee cup and fastidiously conserves creamers, paper, and napkins, the permanent nametag will remind others that they are not as environmentally conscious as they could be. Whether this will irritate or gently humble people remains to be seen, but either way they will likely keep a safe distance from the permanent nametag wearer.

The wrong nametag is much better than no nametag. Join an event at mid-morning break wearing the nametag from another conference. People like to accommodate someone who has jumped ship, if only to vicariously escape from their own conference. The key thing, of course, is that you were on a worthy ship to begin with, not dog-paddling all by yourself, so the "wrong" nametag must be prominent and ideally from one of the following: an accounting convention (the liberated accountant is an appealing archetype, as indicated by the best-selling *Counting the Days to Freedom*); a convention on small tissue management (no one will ask for details); or a symposium on something obscure and scientific (people will be flattered someone so intelligent chose their company). Confess that you've never done anything like this before but couldn't help yourself because something, some force you've never felt before, just drew you. People love the idea of being discovered, especially through supernatural forces, and you will almost certainly be welcomed.

Communication devices

Pagers are easily accessed at medical conventions and political events and are most useful at high security events where one may need to leave a room frequently. They are also fine for simply indicating that you might be needed at any time. Cell phones serve a similar function but are also handy for rushed entrances, where one dashes by registration in the throes of an urgent call. They are found wherever real estate people, surgeons, and other indispensable folk gather.

Small appliances

It is nice to talk into something once in a while, and if you don't have a cell phone, consider a tiny tape recorder. These are most abundant at journalism conferences, but journalists tend to hoard and some are quite alert. I found mine during nap time at a twenty-four-hour playwrighting competition.

Also for the talkers among us, headsets are used by stage managers and sound crews and can be found in television studios, theatres, and film sets. They are vital for those of us who assume a security role from time to time.

Although prevalent at business and legal events, laptop computers are cumbersome and not at all versatile. I don't advise them.

Low-tech

Daytimers are essential to those operating in government circles and are found in board rooms everywhere during morning coffee breaks— between 10 and 10:30 a.m. In my city, daytimer cults have taken hold in government departments (as well as some corporations), and staff log tomes containing charts, schedules, recipes, personal budgets and God knows what else. For convenience, obtain a daytimer of modest size that is already crammed full of appointments and personal notes. Make it distinctively yours by highlighting things in mauve and green (highlighter pens are also widely available in board rooms). Jot down notes to yourself throughout the day, but especially at mealtimes, when it is effective to remember something with a look of alarm, check your schedule, sigh with relief, and ask someone to pass the buns.

A raffle box is ungainly but gives one an official function.

Fundraisers for the symphony and so forth, with their hundred-dollar-a-plate admission, can be tricky to infiltrate, and a good raffle box or drum will often get you in as people are forever eager to win something. Nice metal latticed drums are often located in hospital foyers, especially during United Way campaigns.

Dollies can be found in hotel loading zones, and a person can on occasion roll a couple of boxes into a dining hall or private function and then integrate.

Other parts

Washing

Regular cleansing can be difficult in a hostel environment, and toiletries, should you be fortunate enough to get under a shower, are poor in quality and quantity. Luxurious bathing can be enjoyed in the exclusive fitness facilities of good hotels. Simply sign your name and room number in the book at the desk, and ask if it's a dry sauna, your asthma can act up if there's not enough moisture. The clerk will either reassure you or apologize, and off you go. For a purposeful look, carry a swim bag, or just a bathing suit; these can be obtained at the same time as hosiery (see Hosiery).

Hair

The degree to which one's hair is controlled should approximate the control level of an event. Unrestrained hair is fine at the annual Raku Society's open house, but would make people nervous at either sitting of the Canadian Armed Forces retirement tea.

Wherever there is seated dining, there is structured hair. In terms of volume, big hair may be closer to God in some circles, but in general it aggravates people, taking up altogether too much space and often blocking someone's view. If you must backcomb, exert restraint. As silver is gold according to the celebrity hair guru Shaft, don't bother with dye if you're getting grey. Do find someone with haircutting skill, though, especially if you have curly hair. I am thankful for Marta, formerly known in certain Detroit circles as the Velvet Snipper, now famous here in the west for her mastery with natural curl. Marta does my hair monthly in exchange for a Tarot reading.

For the short term, a shaved head with scarf is effective, cancer recovery being the assumption most people will make. Should someone be so insensitive as to question your registration, respond softly with, *No, I didn't register. My doctor didn't think I'd live this long.*

Make-up

For make-up I use cosmetic counters at the Bay. Cosmetic clerks can be rude, and the head cosmetician at the Bay used to really put me off. The first couple of times she snarled, *Can I help you?* I replied, *Oh no, just looking, thanks.* But one day I said, *Yes, you can. What do you think about this coral lipstick?— Is it too orange? I am a winter.* We looked at each other for a moment. *Well,* she said, *with your colouring I'd stick to true reds.* And she

walked away and left me alone. To be fair to the Bay, they do
have on staff a helpful, pleasant cosmetic clerk who works
weekends and helps me prepare for weddings.

Weddings are the only events I can think of that require a
thick, full face of make-up, natural being the aesthetic everywhere else. A pre-set face puts a wedding party at ease, what
with all the uncertainty of a reception, not to mention the
marriage itself. Go to town with foundation especially, leaving
a line so people can see what trouble you've taken.

More on skin care

As skin is the meeting place for you and your *ogo*, it should be
well attended to. Keeping it tidy with washing and tastefully
decorated with make-up is fine, but skin responds most glow-
ingly to the careful touch of another person. The make-up
counter comes in handy once again. Consult cosmeticians about
products where skin tone matching is important, such as foundation, concealer and powder. They will stroke your cheeks
with various shades, and may go all out and give you a complete
make-over. My ears like lots of attention, so I regularly get my
glasses adjusted by downtown opticians. For feet, one must try
on shoes at the best shoe stores, but even so you might have a
sales clerk who just thumps a box down rather than putting your
feet in the shoes himself. A bra fitting is a lovely experience,
especially in lingerie boutiques where the clerks are attentive

and the dressing rooms plush. There is much strap and closure adjusting, which I find most effective in releasing shoulder tension. Finally, there are massage schools where students need volunteer clients. Don't sign up until close to the end of their term.

Collection

Searching

There are as many sources for one good outfits as there are styles and it is helpful to consider how you might go about getting things together. Each piece of my one good outfit was found in a different location. If you are an experienced thrift store shopper you will know how difficult it is to find one quality item, and you may feel overwhelmed by the challenge of finding up to five different needles in many many haystacks. To reduce that sense of futility I imagined my one good outfit pieces as siblings who had been separated by disaster and were waiting for me to reunite them. We were all looking for each other, in a dramatic search directed more by destiny than by me. It is also helpful to envision a magnetic attraction between you and your *ogo*, to understand that you are energetically attuned to each other. And, as you will learn in Part III— you are.

Sewing

Since needles have just come up we may as well talk about sewing. It's handy to be able to do minor alterations on hems or zippers, and I was grateful for the sewing machine at the hostel so I could shorten my dress. That said, I hope to dissuade all but the most gifted dressmakers among you from remodeling attempts and major alterations such as recutting sleeves, changing a neckline or lapels, or drastic re-sizing. I am thinking of an old school friend who would start with a dress and end with a hairband. Once you start cutting it is hard to stop, and all too soon you have spent a day and still have nothing to wear.

Stealing

If you are in a real rush you may be thinking of getting new garments from stores. Do understand that despair has a strong odour and security staff immediately sense desperate people. If you are confident of your skills, consider the tactic of wearing nothing but shoes, stockings and a trenchcoat (closed) into the store and your *ogo* out. Once you have an outfit, it is possible to trade it in using the same tactic. Overcoats are easy to obtain at downtown coatchecks in convention centres, and in church cloakrooms during services.

After helping yourself in this way, it is thoughtful to leave something behind. At the store, for instance, put coupons or poetry in jacket pockets. In a church cloakroom, a little picture of St. Francis of Assisi taped to the now empty hanger is a nice touch. You never know how much a small offering like this might mean to someone.

I must mention my friend Charmaine, with the Donna Karan wardrobe to die for, all taken from two upscale shops where she is always welcome. She even returned something once, without the bill, of course, and they gave her a refund. The thing about Charmaine is:

1) she is tall and striking, and
2) she used to be rich.

Charmaine and I share a locker at the bus depot but, sadly, we are not the same size. I am always pleased to see her, especially on my low days. Privilege has an uplifting scent, and a whiff of Charmaine perks me right up for the day. Do seek out a previously wealthy *ogoer* if you are a novice *ogoer*, if only to ask for guidance during "entitlement assumption" (see next section).

Shopping

The conventional place to acquire one good outfit is a consignment or thrift store. Wonderful things can be found at Salvation Armies, especially in out-of-the-way stores. For every fifty square feet of thrift store space there is one "find," according to studies on the matter, so the best strategy is to cover as much ground as possible. Try to work intuitively, to sense quality rather than search for it, and you will be able to move quickly through the racks. Whenever I am coming close to something good in a thrift shop my throat develops a tickle and I stop and look.

Serendipity

As with most things, personal connections are valuable. You may know someone who cleans houses for women your size with walk-in closets. If you are of a certain age, acquaintances may be going through mid-life transformations which generally involve new wardrobes.

Post-divorce purges are very promising. Large theatres can also be excellent sources for good clothing, especially if they do a lot of modern plays. The costume department and storage are most accessible during dress rehearsals, and the larger the cast the easier it is to explore unnoticed.

I am hoping you now have a picture of your one good outfit and an idea of how you are going to get it together. Both the outfit and its assembly rely on planning, serendipity and instinct— the same things required for effective mobilization.

Pre-operative preparations

Entitlement assumption

I've said that my outfit is only a collection of parts without me. Now that we're ready for the how-to's of wearing one good outfit, I will expand this claim to say "without me *and my sense of entitlement.*" Any outfit will droop, weak and dejected, without the support of a self-assured body. Take a few moments to observe people and their clothing and you will see what I mean. I am in the foyer of a high-end shopping centre, and there are many people going by with clothes that cost the earth but look like hell. Here is a woman in a Givenchy knit dress, silk-cashmere and deep aubergine, a regal dress for someone with regal bearing. With her strained face and collapsed chest, this poor woman might as well be wearing a hospital gown. Now here comes someone in a Debrille suit, chin and chest thrust forward so far that her body and its outfit follow like a child's pull toy. All around me there are many more outfits that shrink from or strain against misaligned bodies. Putting good clothes over poor posture, as Neuni said, is like putting uphol-stery over rotting wood— why cover it at all?

This is not to lecture you on proper carriage. When I tried

to straighten my back after twenty-five years of stooping it was painful and not at all constructive. If you too have had a long slump, be especially gentle. It is much better to assume entitlement through absorption rather than force. The best places for this assumption are lobbies and sitting areas in grand hotels. The grand hotel in my centre was built for British tourists who liked to come to Canada to feel rugged and superior. The lobby was continually filled with people who had too much self-assurance and entitlement, and the excess is still in the air waiting to be inhaled by those of us with entitlement deficiency. I sit in one of the dark green armchairs, plant both feet in a square on the green and rose carpet, take out my daytimer, and breathe deeply. I soak in the richness of the wood, the upholstery, the sumptuous aplomb of it all, and let it reassure me. I let myself be stretched up by the tall windows and high plaster ceiling. I look the founding fathers straight in the eye (they are portrayed in one big bunch over the fireplace) and imagine being among them, helping myself to sandwiches and coffee, expressing strong opinions about the nation's future. It is a knack, this entitlement thing, and it took me a few tries before I felt my spine extend, my chest expand, and my eyes settle.

Non-absorbency issues

If life has been difficult, as it tends to be, you may have had to develop a very thick skin. Absorption will still occur, but it does take more concentration and time. If, however, after four

sittings of about twenty minutes each you still feel no entitlement whatsoever, do consider a little ritual to speed things
along. Something with a filter would be apt. Perhaps you can
make a cup of coffee and, as the coffee drips, envision yourself
extracting the rich flavour of privilege.

Renewal

If there is still no effect, symbolic rebirth is probably the best
route. When one can't assume entitlement in mid-life, one
might as well go back to the beginning, so to speak, and claim
it as a birthright. Rebirth rituals vary in terms of complexity,
the most simple being a long shower in a dimly lit room.
Essentially, a rebirth involves moving wetly from a dark small
space to a light open area. If you want to explode into your new
life with a big splash, then velocity is important, and you might
try water slides. These can be found in large malls, outdoor
recreation areas, and a few hotels. The cashier will usually let
you in if you explain that your child forgot his antibiotics.

For a more contemplative experience, I suggest a car wash.
My friend Emily Drake, whose former partner was in car sales,
pioneered the carwash method. Although she did not yet feel
entitled to much, she did know how auto sales worked and was
able to test drive a Cavalier after asking the right questions. She
drove it to a busy car wash, got the access number by watching
the driver in front of her punch it in, and drove through when
it was her turn. Being very literal, Emily removed her one good

outfit as soon as she was safely inside the carwash, then snapped the seat back, and turned around so she was lying head first as the car rumbled through. There's something to be said for real life enactments, but I do have a safety concern with the head and neck positioned this way. A woman at an internal auditors' conference last week was wearing a neck brace because the person behind her in a carwash had gone in too soon, and bumped her all the way through.

Once you have been reborn, entitlement assumption will occur very quickly. A brief sitting in the right lobby will be sufficient.

Building an image

With a bit of entitlement under her belt, the *ogoer* is ready to master projection. One projects entitlement so others understand one has it and behave in respectful ways that add to it, so more can be projected and so on. It works much like the nitrogen cycle. Projection is best learned by imitation, and excellent role models for *ogoers* can be found in exclusive clothing stores. Since it is necessary for sales staff to match exorbitant merchandise without outshining their customers, they must be both elite and ordinary, the paradoxical combination at the heart of *ogoing*. We, too, must exude privilege, prosperity, ease, and good judgement without being distinctive (except for contrasters— see next section). And, just as the sales clerks' savvy to some extent hides their monetary dependence, just as their inadequate salaries and unpaid bills are nowhere evident in their being, so too must our material concerns be undetectable.

When I was a novice *ogoer*, my inspiration was Yvonne, footwear specialist at Holts. Shoes, by the way, are the first and often the only thing clerks look at when you come into their stores. Because I had not yet found my good shoes, Yvonne did not bother to look above my ankles, and I was able to frequent her department and observe her comportment. Using the three-way mirror in the lingerie department, I practised her walk, hand gestures, and standing pose until my body had fully registered these motions. With a close facial study, I approximated her expression of self-worth by performing other, simple exercises to activate cheekbones, expand the temples, and release the chin and forehead. Once I had all this under control, and was wearing my entire good outfit, Yvonne began interacting with me, and over the years we have become friends. Lately I have been able to reciprocate her guidance, inadvertently given though it may have been, by advising her on an independent business venture.

To blend or to contrast

While selecting and refining your image there is an important issue to consider. Are you the type to stand out in a crowd? Or do you easily blend into most groups? Most of us are blenders and can further develop that capacity with our *ogos*. The challenge is to refine our neutrality. For distinctive people, or contrasters, blending is not an option. Contrasters must convey blasé superiority in order to be highlights rather than misfits wherever they go. Think of the contrasting trim that vitalizes an outfit, the bright scarf that "makes" a navy dress. Because difference is popular now, and everyone wants to be the trim rather than the foundation, contrasters do get a break from time to time. Some events are so full of people being unique that contrasters can blend right in and relax.

Specialization

Although we are getting into operational matters here, contrasting people must think about specializations at this early stage. A conspicuous *ogoer* must appear to have a purpose. To start with, think of an appealing occupational field which could explain your presence just about anywhere. Examples include security, journalism, data collection, lighting or sound technology, environmental engineering, and espionage. To learn what catchphrases and functional accessories to use, find someone who actually works in the field and engage them in a chat about anything at all. They will be sure to use an acronym or two specific to their occupation, as well as certain gestures. To be an engineer, for instance, you should mention "chillers," "the bin method" and ASHRAY every once in a while, and play with change or keys in your pocket.

Specializations are handy for blenders, too, but can be

learned in later operational stages. It is doubtlessly more difficult for the novice contraster than the new blender, as she must be something of a shining star right off the bat. On the positive side, contrasters become highly skilled in a short time, in what is known as telescoped development. Within the first two years of operations, compared to an average of six years for most blenders, three contrasters in my area achieved universal access— the ability to, as Leona puts it, go anywhere you damn well feel like any time you damn well want.

A contraster

Roberta Elders is six feet three inches and black. She has decided to be an event organizer, and carries a clipboard and pager. The desk staff at the convention centre and at the main hotels assume she is management, and whenever she appears they check with her to make sure things are okay. People generally try to please her, but her high profile also ensures occasional conflicts. At the First Ministers' conference on health care, for instance, where supper was to be a gala and succulent affair, she was asked point-blank for security access, and had to retreat. In June, at the counter-intelligence conference, a group of angry spies blamed Roberta for unwelcome media attendance and were dead set on getting her fired. Thankfully the manager happened to be off having a glucose tolerance test. Apart from these awkward incidents, Roberta's specialty works well for her. She

enjoys a varied gourmet diet, and has developed a strong base of contacts, so she will smoothly branch into another field when the time is right.

A blender

Teresa had a highly diversified blender operation until she, quite by accident, discovered sports reporting in the Westin Hotel lobby one Tuesday morning. It was Tall Tuesday, the annual draft pick for the National Women's Basketball League, and the lobby was squished full of reporters and players. Teresa jumped into the fray, for the body contact more than anything, eventually finding herself nose to chest with Phoebe McQueen, the Winnipeg Whips' gifted centre. Phoebe and Teresa hit it off rather well and Teresa developed a passion for basketball and other sports along with a certain status in sports reporting, having invented *Sporte Internazionale*, an Italian wire service, with herself as foreign correspondent.

Without wanting to detract from Teresa's success, I must say that high profile positions do make *ogoing* awkward, especially for blenders, who really forfeit their blending capacity when they assume visible roles in the media. Ideally, a blender can have a nice discreet specialty in something like pharmacy while maintaining diversified operations. That said, Teresa continues to do splendidly and is in no danger of missing a meal.

Mutual interest

Every *ogo* has its history, its story to tell, and it will grace your body with so much more care if you know and appreciate that history. Gina Louise, somewhat obsessive in my opinion, extremely thorough in hers, is an expert on textile manufacturing and marketing. She learned the history of her good outfit by researching the factory where each piece was made, the origins of the fabric, and so forth.

I took a more personal, sensory approach and tried to get impressions of my outfit's experience. I wore it directly on my skin (no slip, etc.), while standing in the spacious rotunda at the art gallery. With some concentration, I sensed, one by one, all those who had contributed to the creation of my one good outfit: the designer who stole the design from one of his students; the fabric makers and dyers; the cutters and sewers, in particular Brenda who was anguished about her three-year-old's behaviour (he was in a biting phase); the buyer for Macy's, who almost rejected my dress because it reminded her of her sister, whom she hated; Zola Mackle, a sales clerk who sold my dress to Rachel MacKinnon, who wanted something discreet and classic for the opening of a suburban library named in honour of her uncle; and Rachel's cousin Mariette, who could have had a brilliant future had she thought of using the dress for an *ogo*, but didn't, sadly, and wore it to job interviews instead. When Mariette became sick with ovarian cancer the dress and her other clothes (most of them also supplied by Rachel) were given to the Goodwill and put on the shelves by Ron and Melva Spakes, whom I know and am fond of. The rotunda, as you can imagine, was crowded with the presence of my good outfit acquaintances, and I felt it relax on my body as I became familiar with them.

Integration

As Leslie says, we are porous creatures. She came to realize this while recovering from the serious depression that struck her after the first outing in her *ogo*. Without consciously trying to explore her outfit's past, she had merely absorbed it, and its history was hideous. Pieced together by one worker who only did sleeves, another who only did pockets, and so on, each weaving her own worries into the garment, it was a beautiful dress but heavy with sadness. Leslie's depression began to lift once she was receptive to her garment's history, painful as it was to realize, and she really improved after devising an integration ritual in which each piece had an opportunity to express itself. The sleeves hung with the exhaustion of Marta P., who had basted three hundred and twenty sleeves into as many armholes six days a week for nine years, and knew she would continue doing so until she died, which could not be soon, as her daughters were only four and eleven. The welt pockets released the boredom of one woman who attached the linings and welts, and pain from the presser who was clumsy and burned herself frequently with the industrial iron. And on it went, until everything, including seam binding and interfacing, had unravelled its past and released every fibre from pain.

Do consider Leslie's approach if you need to relieve the scattered, fractured kind of despair a pieced-together outfit can produce. I also advise a tailor-made ritual as the whole idea is to acknowledge the distinctive experience of your outfit. Your ritual need not be complex— start with circular arm motions and something appropriate will quickly develop.

A cling-free bond

Once you have a sense of each other, your outfit and you can begin exploring your relationship in more depth. There is a certain amount of sneering that goes on when I talk of rapport-building. Certainly you cannot idly get to know your outfit while your hair falls out from protein deficiency, but you will find that the inevitable problems of operations become more manageable once the relationship dynamics have been attended to. Interdependence is a tricky thing and it's wise to clarify the terms of your partnership. If one partner becomes over-reliant on the other or starts taking the other for granted as often happens in these relationships, disharmony develops and *ogoing* is unquestionably impaired. Ideally there are both mutual support and respectful boundaries; although skin and fabric are porous and continually exchanging information and particles, they also separate one's body from one's outfit. For both parties to stay on their toes, so to speak, that division must be valued as much as your shared objective.

Questions to ponder:

1) Will you have a lead/follow dynamic? Will you follow your *ogo* as it interacts with other outfts? (See Marcie Hipman's *Surrender for Control: How to Follow Your Clothing* and J.R. Jenning's important *The Directive Dress*.) Or, will you direct its course? (There are many experts on this approach, including Mrs. Sheffield-Dann and Shirley Meranskew.)

2) Do you hope to be fused as one with your outfit? (In some respects, the toughest way to go, but also the ultimate *ogo* experience. Dolly Jamieson perfectly embodies this method and R.J. Matichuk renders it poetically in *Within a Lining*.)

3) Will your outfit represent you, act as your agent, or protect you as a shield? If it is a filter between the world and you, how porous do you want it to be?

4) What about commitment? (You can hardly expect an outfit to transform your life if you plan to ditch it next season.)

Harmonized purpose

Whatever dynamic you choose— and many of us experiment with several— the heightened awareness you and your outfit have of one another will help you be a top-notch team. You will not, in other words, be dragged down or sabotaged by unrecognized needs or issues on either side. A conscious relationship makes for a cutting edge operation, with you and your *ogo* using all sorts of innovations to access promising meals. Pure harmony doesn't happen right off the bat for most of us, although there are exceptions. I am reminded of Dolly Jamieson, who found her outfit after a long, tortured search of thirty-nine days, a record in these parts. Dolly thought she had scoured every second-hand store in the city, when, on the fortieth day, resting in a bus shelter, she saw this sign: Wendy's lothing, and, being a phonetic speller, wondered what Wendy loathed, then wondered if her own self-loathing could be appeased by Wendy, as it was, at that very moment, acute. At the entrance, Dolly stepped over the fallen "C" and inside, found no Wendy. The store was empty except for one slate-coloured Burberry suit hanging, luminescently, on the only hook of the changing room door.

Dolly says she knew, right there in the dressing room, that her grey suit and she were made for each other, and in four and a half years they've never had a problem. For most of us, though, this kind of bond takes three months to create and ongoing receptivity to maintain. Be patient and understand that every time you have a niggly irritation with your outfit you have an opportunity to deepen your partnership.

Moving on

Your guiding light

You have almost completed the *ogo* preparatory stage and will soon spring into operations. Our progression so far has been methodical and sensible, much like a museum tour, and here you are back at the front doors knowing a good deal more than when you started. Once we go outside, though, into the operational wilderness, as Vera St. James calls it, we no longer move from one frame to another in a neat, orderly fashion. Things will seem chaotic and perhaps overwhelming in the initial weeks of operations. Your objective may become unclear or even questionable, and strain between you and your *ogo* may develop. To ease this situation you must firmly hold in your mind a clear concept of elegance. While eating is your objective, elegance is your guiding light.

After convincing the Westin's manager to make what I thought were improvements to the lobby, I was criticized by other *ogoers* and came to realize that the aesthetic criteria for elegance are diverse. Raina Raleigh adores plastic plants, for example, and Sonya D. calls the Westin's recently removed pastel landscape an *important piece*. Although there may be no consensus on what elegance looks like, there is less agreement on how to explain it. Despite my attempts to make it more apparent, I do not presume to know, definitively, what elegance is. Many veteran *ogoers* reflect daily on its nature, and have come to think of elegance not as something one acquires, but as a quality that emerges once one's clutter is removed. Becoming elegant, it seems, is a lifelong practice of embracing life in all its perplexing entirety, while being increasing selective about one's wardrobe.

Because, as *Town and Country* has noted, "elegance is understood by a relatively small percentage of people," *ogoers* have a public-education mandate. Along with *Town and Country*, we can help people accept that "less is not only more— it is also more elegant. In addition to being confused with excess, elegance is also misunderstood as self-display. Nina Griscom hit the nail on the head when she talked about elegance *implying* life experience but "not letting people know how hard things can be." Elegance is about having a lovely calm surface under which a stratum of experience can be glimpsed, a layer where suffering and strength have been mixed in just the right amounts. It is informed, well nourished hope. To keep this in mind, I rely on Dilburt's definition:

Elegance is joyful covering. Elega, after all, means joy (from the Elegas of northern Italy who had seventy-three words in their language for "happy" and none for "sad") and nince *is a rare, exquisite crocus, which*

covered Elega lands every spring. Eleganince *was anglicized to* elegance *in the seventeenth century.*
—Jason Dilburt, *The Happy Elegas* (1991)

Be joyfully covered, then, whatever nuances elegance takes on for you, and whatever your taste in interior décor may be. Be joyfully covered and you will be prepared for anything.

PART II: *OGO* OPERATIONS

Ogo operations

A typical day

On Tuesday, I had breakfast at a film conference. Excellent coffee, juices and a nice assortment of pastries and muffins were provided at a break in their morning workshop. In what remained of the session, I was able to pick up quite a bit about marketing short films. (Break time, between 10:00 and 11:00 a.m., is the best time to join a conference, by the way— just mill about and help yourself.)

For lunch, I joined teachers at their annual conference in the Westin and was among several people who had lost or forgotten their lunch tickets. I ruffled my daytimer, felt my jacket pocket, said, Oh darn, where did *I put that thing?* and continued into the banquet hall with a social studies teacher who felt high school students should have to volunteer in inner city agencies and even sleep on the street a night or so to really understand poverty. I couldn't win the door prize without a ticket, but then I didn't have to face a classroom on Monday morning, either.

For dessert, which the Westin frankly fails at, I went to the Hilton, where a power lunch for businesswomen was underway. The keynote speaker, a well known filmmaker, made the peach cobbler all the more enjoyable with her account of travelling in India. She told us she learned to fold a sari properly because Indian women would pull her into their homes when she didn't have it folded right, and insistently refold it. She said this had been very embarrassing one hot day when she wasn't wearing underwear.

Before supper, I freshened my face at the Bay's cosmetic counter, then decided to forego the film festival's hospitality suite for a dinner buffet at the International Pedway Planners Convention. Entering as the mayor's welcoming address was ending, I joined a table of shiny young men, who, sensitive to the under-representation of women in the room, understood that my presence made them look more progressive than their colleagues, and so were grateful and reluctant to question my credentials. We discussed the busker issue, most of my table-mates favouring buskers for the colour and contour they add to pedways. When someone began to go into Vancouver's busker by-laws at length I returned to the exceptional salad bar for seconds. A middle-aged man was using the salad tongs, first, to poke at artichoke hearts, then hatefully squeeze a marinated mushroom. *What is all this crap?* he snarled, *Where's the pickles, the olives, goddamn bacon bits?* and noticing my chest, *Where's your nametag?* My heart stopped, but I put my plate down, my hand out, introduced myself, and with a steady look at his tag said, *What a pleasure, I've heard so much about you.* Thankfully a waiter came to replenish the crudités, and I could ask her if the dried fruit was sulfured, was there EDTA in the bamboo shoots, and so on, until the angry man commanded her to get hot gravy for his roast beef. I returned to my table with relief, briefly mused over the next day's schedule, and bid my tablemates a warm good night.

Sites

What's out there

A typical *ogo* day is uncertain, surprising, and different from the day before, so don't expect your days to be anything like the one I just described. It is only a sample of what may be enjoyed. This unpredictability is off-putting at first, especially for those with nine-to-five pasts, but have faith. It's not as if *ogoers* aimlessly drift about waiting for things to happen. We do have coordinates. The uncertainty is not one big void but a series of surprises, each boxed, so to speak, in a fixed location. The more familiar you are with these locations, the more finesse you'll have in responding to whatever pops up inside them. Your *ogo* operations should begin, then, with a map of *ogoable* sites, central sites being those that are big, close by, and home to a variety of events. In the margins are places that infrequently hold catered events, and/or are difficult to get to. An example of such a map is provided below.

A matrix of sites

Airport, pilot's lounge	Ishwood Gallery	Central Pentecostal
Healy Ford	St. Peter's Basilica	Empress Line Hospitality Centre
City Centre Concert Hall	PanPacific Trading HQ	Hilton Hotel
Convention Centre	Petroleum Club	King's College
City Centre Art Gallery	Regency Hotel	Westin Ballroom
City Hall	Main Stage Theatre	University, Faculty Club
Inland Cement HQ	Real Estate Council of AB	General Hospital
Legislature MLA lounge	Dow Chemical HQ	Peak Drilling Training Centre

Transportation

Although most sites in an *ogoer's* matrix will be centrally located and within easy walking distance from each other, a few, such as the airport, will require transportation. You might arrange rides during your chats at conventions; sooner or later someone will say, "Why don't you tag along with me?" after you muse "Gee, I guess I should figure out how to get to the airport." Or, you might join a group outside of one of the better hotels as they get on their airport shuttle. (Ensure that the van or bus is, in fact, going to the airport and not to West Edmonton Mall or, as in Anita Shirlee's case last month, a casino on the outskirts of Boyle.) A return trip from the airport should be timed with the arrival of a full flight from a faraway place. Join the disembarked passengers as they come out of Customs, and head for Arrivals where at least one person will be holding a sign with a stranger's name on it. Often you will see two or three signs, and you can choose who you would like to be.

Sites and size

Medium-sized centres of about one million people, including three or four satellite communities, are ideal for one good outfit operations, as there are enough amenities and not too much competition for them. The larger a city is, the harder it is to feel special or safe, so people go to great lengths to make their events exclusive and secure. *Ogoers* certainly operate in Montreal, Dallas and other large cities, but they put up with a lot more than we have to in, say, Edmonton. In queen-sized centres such as Tokyo and New York, one simply chooses a mid-sized area to operate in. Always choose your territory in geographic, not social terms. That is, don't try to operate only in the arts or only among business people. Regardless of a city's size, homogenous social and occupational groups are never big enough— you will get tired of the same people, and they will get tired of you. Many challenges face the *ogoer* in the petite centre of less than half a million people, as one will become conspicuous within nine to thirteen months. A contrasting *ogoer*, who is conspicuous right off the bat, cannot operate in petite centres.

A chart of ogoable sites

(Figures reflect the estimated number of places that merit *ogoer* attention, not the total number of sites in any given centre.)

Population	academic inst.	business (i.e., hotels)	arts centres	political inst.	churches
>3 million	1-3	9-12	3-7	4-7	12
>1 million	1-2	6-10	4	3-5	8
>500,000	1-2	4-8	3	2-4	5
>100,000	1	3-5	1	2	4
>50,000	1	2	1	1-2	2

Sectors

Types of events

Simply charting locations is unlikely to provide you with a sense
of the range of activities you may encounter. While some sites
determine the nature of events they contain, others hold a wide
variety of unrelated functions. Rather than grouping events by
location, then, *ogoers* divide them according to the occupational
or social field they represent. There are six main sectors for most
ogo operations. In an effort to expand your sense of possibility,
I have used these to loosely categorize everything I attended
this April.

> *Academic:*
> Faculty of Commerce awards gala
> Professor Stanley's retirement banquet
> "Diatoms and Eurtrophication" seminar and lunch
> Hydrocarbon conference
>
> *Business:*
> Texaco staff retreat
> Bank of Nova Scotia employee recognition dinner

The Tao of Takeovers workshop with lunch
Stellix annual shareholders buffet
Radio Shack convention
Conflicts with No Losers seminar with lunch

Arts:
Annual Printmakers' Awards
Streetcar opening night
Annual Public Library fundraiser
Radiance magazine launch
Opening of Turkle exhibition
Kodaly Conference for music educators
Jane Austen Society Tea

Politics:
Anti-MAI post-rally dinner
Board of Governors gala
Premier's appreciation dinner for Business Against
        Healthcare (BAH)
BAH appreciation dinner for premier
Meet the Liberal leadership candidates brunch

Religious:
Easter brunch at St. Mary's
Bishop George ordination and reception
Persephone Rising festival
Sacred dance competition
Pat and Roberta's handfasting ceremony

Social/Family/Misc.:
Bon voyage party for Leo
Classes of '72-'75, Ponoka Nurses Reunion
Kiwanis Annual Dinner and Dance
Macnab family reunion
Australian Coaching Awards Dinner
High Fidelity: the couples conference
Scrabble Invitational
Wildlife Photography Awards and Banquet
Powersurge convention
Tomley-Pisner wedding reception
Financial Planning for Women Seminar and lunch

Field notes

Academia and business

Increasingly, academic and business fields overlap so that a person is often in both at the same time. For a thorough analysis of this phenomenon, see L.L. Knott's *Plato Drank Pepsi, Socrates Preferred Coke: Real Thingness in the Academy*. For our purposes, it is useful to know that for one reason or another both fields must appear to be accessible. In either, speak of permeable boundaries and flux. In terms of socializing, be conscious of eye movement. One often looks upward at corporate functions to make spiritual references (see *Jesus Is a CEO* by Laurie B. Jones, or the *Zen of Success* by Judy Jacks). At academic events, one talks about grounding this or that in good research, and perodically gazes downward to say, *But where's the body?*

While business events are abundantly catered, one has to hunt for food at post-secondary institutions. For those of you who will be attending the university in my area, I can recommend graduate student music recitals, the Board of Governors' Christmas Party, anything in Pharmacy, and the annual Poultry Science barbecue.

Arts

Mid-sized cities generally have a concert hall, a large theatre, and a major public art gallery, all of which have catered galas, charity events, and openings of one kind or another. As indicated earlier, raffle drums come in handy at these places, as do floral arrangements and other centerpieces one can barge through a crowd with. A press pass works well at arts events, but remember, if you use one, to look interested in the performers. At opening night receptions, usually held in the theatre foyer, don't waste any time getting to the food trays. Theatre people are always hungry.

Charity functions and fundraisers can be a fine source of elegant food if they are organized by gay men (any age) or women over forty-five (any orientation). The same applies to art openings. Otherwise, expect medium cheddar and boxed wine.

Investigate arts festivals in your city. Aside from all the catered parties and hospitality platters I enjoyed at the summer jazz festival in my centre, I finally learned to appreciate acid jazz.

Politics: making the most of an election

There are many free lunches to be had in the political arena, but good food is most abundant during election campaigns. To be dined, you might represent a taxpayers' association or take on another lobbyist specialization. You might also roam among campaign offices to see which candidates best feed their volunteers. Don't miss the victory celebrations for whoever wins, or the follow-up dinners for volunteers and supporters.

Religion: finding a church that fits

It is important to find a church that fits your weekend and holiday needs, as these can be challenging times for quality, nutritious food. Look for a large, well-heeled congregation. A good mix of old people and young adults is necessary for upcoming funeral and wedding receptions. Ethnic diversity can mean that a variety of feast days are celebrated, but it can also mean that fasting is practised on occasion. Ideally one can rotate among two or three appropriate churches, hitting feasts and missing famines.

Formerly belonging to a religion that encouraged lots of reproduction, Deirdre Miller has three children and is familiar with church operations. She has created potluck steering committees in eleven parishes, with many dinners and occasional retreats being the happy result. United Churches, she advises, generally offer the best balance of good food and short services, but one must shop around, as United Churches vary tremendously as far as social action, income levels, and food preferences go. Certainly you want to avoid congregations that over-donate to social causes and can't afford to bring interesting food to potlucks.

Family and social functions

In my experience, informal functions take far more energy, as they demand intensified interpersonal exchanges. One has to show interest, listen closely, and emote. Check the paper for weddings, funerals, family reunions, and other gatherings outside of your own parish or equivalent. Also consider convocation parties for university students in May and high school graduation dinners in June. Go as late as possible to any social event, as food is generally slow to be served, given the focus on relating.

Hospitals

There will be one downtown hospital in your mid-sized centre, and although it will not likely provide you with fabulous dining, it can be a good bread-and-butter pit stop. Primary food sources, in ascending order of appeal, are patient meal trays, the staff cafeteria, retirement teas, hospital rounds sponsored by pharmaceutical firms, administrative lunches, and the annual Christmas party for the board of directors. If a medical specialization is appealing, you can pretty well choose whatever role you like, given acute staff shortages in healthcare facilities. Surgical garb and other uniforms can be found in laundry services in the basement.

I know of *ogoers* who find hospital visits deeply fulfilling. Margaret has always been fascinated by comas, her husband having been in one for seven years before finally passing away, and she was happy to locate several comatose patients and order food for them. Every night, Margaret enjoys supper at the hospital, rotating among her comatose acquaintances, reading them passages from Dante.

Strategic planning

Needs assessment

For contrasting *ogoers*, planning is essential. You should use your matrix of sites to map weekly rotation schedules for at least the first six months of operations. Otherwise, you will likely become too familiar in central locales.

For blenders, planning is fine in moderation. It can get out of hand, though, as the fanatical time management movement shows. With dismay I have watched the daytimers of certain blenders in my centre expand from pocket to toaster size, and I can only hope that their spontaneity skills have not proportionately shrunk. One *ogoer* actually made money so she could fill in the budget sections of her organizer, bought food to fill in the shopping list sections, put all our birthdays in the back, and, for the business card section, took the raffle box from Earl's restaurant. To prevent this sort of extremism, gratify your planning urges only after you have overindulged at a meal. Scheduling not only helps one digest, it balances that overstuffed sensation with feelings of discipline.

Building an information base

The insider edge: hey-yous

A note must be made on those people whose work is in the same spirit as our own, although it takes a different form. They also operate independently throughout various institutions, but instead of using an *ogo* as a passport they rely on uniforms. "Any uniform at all" is their motto, so *ogoers* first called them *a.u.a.a.s* which was quickly shortened to *a.u.s* and then became *hey-yous*, as that is how uniformed people are so often addressed. The main difference between *hey-yous* and *ogoers* seems to be the *hey-you* preference for solitude versus the *ogoers'* taste for social interaction. Most *hey-yous* are acutely sensitive people who can practically hear the grass growing. They would suffer in noisy banquet halls, and the neutral expression so integral to *ogoers* would be impossible for them to sustain. Those of us who have been in *ogos* for some time have come to know several *hey-yous* well, and you may have heard us greet them with a friendly, *Hey you! Call me a cab.*

Hey-yous operate within large institutions, including hotels, by getting a uniform and assuming the appropriate occupational role. In a hotel, chambermaid uniforms afford maximum freedom of movement and access, whereas in hospitals, the brown overalls of maintenance workers give one the most liberty. To move among several institutions, *hey-yous* use a generic uniform signifying security guard, paramedic, or religious figure (i.e., monk or minister). The latter is best for those with small appetites and a peaceful demeanour; even so, people around them become uncomfortable or confessional, according to Phoebe K., *hey-you* expert. Although she had many longstanding *hey-you* roles, Phoebe wore a clerical collar for only one day, during which she heard about a Bank of Montreal clerk's embezzlement (at the banks' Employee Recognition Breakfast at Providence Centre); the adulterous thoughts of a yoga teacher (same site; the Alberta Healers' Association's luncheon); and the homicidal urges of a paramedic (Grey Nuns Hospital cafeteria).

Chambermaid uniforms and brown overalls are more popular as they allow *hey-yous* to keep to themselves and eat in peace.

Interfacing with hey-yous

Apart from being kindred spirits, *hey-yous* are an *ogoer's* most valuable source of insider information. I have established long-term relationships with three *hey-yous* who now let me know about upcoming galas, VIP receptions, and other unpublicized events where excellent refreshments will be featured. In return, I take them as guests to functions where my status is secure, save delicacies from events they cannot access, and intervene whenever they are rudely treated by managers or guests. It is not an equal relationship— clearly I gain more than do my *hey-you* friends. But they are very generous, and for the most part like to see *ogoers* operate with ease. Once you have been in operations for a while, you will develop a sixth sense for *hey-yous*, and they will know you, too.

Over the years, *hey-yous* have advanced me menus for upcoming banquets, provided security codes and badges for high-level government functions, and arranged for me to use suites when I wanted to host a function myself, or just have a little quiet time.

There are a few gifted, energetic individuals who play both *hey-you* and *ogo* roles. I recall, at one of the Premier's banquets for business last year, the stellar performance of Phoebe Katz, who served the raspberry parfait after enjoying four courses as a representative of her Society for the Advancement of Indigo. Stationed for the most part in our city's best downtown hotel as a tour guide in period costume, Phoebe makes the entire third floor available to *ogoers* for New Year's, and keeps emergency rooms open when the hostel gets full. Many of us are grateful to her. Phoebe is working on a guidebook along the lines of my own *One Good Outfit* for *hey-yous*, and Delores and I have been pleased to provide editing and production resources.

Other insider sources

Although *hey-yous* are incomparable in their skill and knowledge, there are other friendly insiders who can provide useful information. For instance, ever since we discovered our common fascination with old soap operas when the *As the World Turns* retrospective and reunion was held there in June, the doorman at the Westin always lets me know about interesting guests. *You'll never guess who got in today,* he'll say as he swings open the glass door. Then he tells me the press conference or reception details. For the most part, it is best to stay invisible to administrative staff in hotels and other institutions, especially registration clerks, who can be suspicious to the point of psychosis. Those working as doormen, chambermaids and porters, however, are often less rule-bound, and more informed. They may be aware of *hey-yous* among them, and may well know what you are up to as well. Once someone starts looking familiar to you, acknowledge them with that nod of professional brotherhood used in medical and legal gatherings, and after a while add an open-ended greeting, such as, *Seems quiet,* or *Lots going on today.* If they are aware of your operations, and want to be helpful, they will respond with specific information. *Yes, it is busy— a banquet for the foresters in the Bilbo Room at 5:30; the Shemsky family reunion in Wildrose at 6:00, and a jazz quartet and light buffet downstairs at 8:00.* Do not become dependent on hotel staff for information. Chat infrequently, as they could get in trouble for socializing on the job. Their supervisor will be the housekeeping manager, who is likely to be autocratic and unpleasant.

Postings in hotels

Hotels post the major events of the day in a visible place on the main floor. This makes things much easier for us than walking into crowded ballrooms without a clue. The convention centre in my city has a flashing sign over the escalators, so you can see what's happening as you descend into the conference area. Although these postings are helpful, don't come to rely on them as your primary guides on where to go. In medium-sized centres, there are only five or six main downtown hotels with worthwhile functions at which to dine, and if you are rotating among them on a daily basis you will become overly familiar to even the most unobservant desk clerks.

Hotel frequency ratios

According to a recent study on the matter, one should not appear in the same hotel more than once every ten days in the first year of operations, once every fifteen days after one year of operations, and once every twenty-two days after two years. These figures are based on the current low staff-turnover rates in hotels and other centres. Perhaps if the employment situation improves, hotel staff will become transient once again and *ogoers* will have less need to be so careful. For the time being, though, limit yourself to three different hotels per week, visiting each during a different shift. A hotel rotation chart is an excellent safety mechanism, and might look like this:

Week 1	M.	T.	W.	T.	F.	S.	S.
Westin	EM[1]						
Four Seasons		L[2]					
Chateau Lacombe					D[3]		
Howard Johnson Plaza							
Hotel MacDonald							

Week 2	M.	T.	W.	T.	F.	S.	S.
Westin							
Four Seasons							
Chateau Lacombe				MM[4]			
Howard Johnson Plaza						L	
Hotel MacDonald		D					

Week 3	M.	T.	W.	T.	F.	S.	S.
Westin			L				
Four Seasons						D	
Chateau Lacombe							
Howard Johnson Plaza							
Hotel MacDonald		MM					

1 Early morning snack, generally available during conference registration.

2 Lunch

3 Dinner

4 Mid-morning snack, offered during session breaks.

Becoming an information centre

Finding information on events involves much less legwork
when the information comes to you. This will not happen until
you have been in operations for some time, and have access to
a fax, e-mail and other tools, but it is something you can happily
anticipate and work towards. Office access is easiest in government departments, particularly in the health sector, where so
many employees are medicated for depression and anxiety that
a new face is scarcely noticed. Go into an office as soon as it
re-opens after lunch; most of the staff won't have returned yet.
Busy yourself at a computer, do not look up as people go by,
and if anyone does ask, say that you are checking the tracking
system. I favour a small government-funded addiction agency.
The high rate of long-term disability leaves among staff means
that there is always a vacant office, and from time to time I am
happy to help out with counselling clients.

Media representative

Media representatives are supplied with more information than
they know what to do with and you might consider being a
columnist for, say, *Transcend: The Magazine for Those a Notch
Above*, or *Abundance*, or some such thing. At your next well-
heeled event, jot down quick notes in a small coiled pad, appear
interested in people, look stressed, and when people ask, say

you're a correspondent for _____. Pause for a second, and with a wry half-smile, explain it's out of New Haven or New Mexico, the target being people with conscious wealth. Confide that it's not selling terribly well here, but you know it could, and offer your business card as you tell your listener she looks like the perfect contact person.

In general, one can receive all kinds of information about upcoming events if one provides the right kind of service: communications, catering and a speakers' bureau are the most common. In the latter case, one leaves brochures around advertising a range of published, accredited experts of one kind or another who speak on any number of fashionable topics. From time to time you may get a request that is hard to turn down, but unless you are a contraster with a motivational speaker specialty, do exert some self-restraint and remain inconspicuous.

Society newsletters

Newsletters or circulars can also be useful information gathering tools, especially for those with specializations. Teresa, for instance, has a sports reporting specialty— as you may recall— and she continually receives event notices for her Sports Writers' Association of the Prairies (SWAP) newsletter. Follow Teresa's example and use a simple format with classic masthead. On the back page have a calendar of events, and on the cover a report on some lavish affair. If the target audience is discriminating, and if you have a second fax or answering machine, mention the brilliant catering by, let's say, Chez Flan, and provide their number. When people call to make bookings, you will be informed of select functions not otherwise advertised, before you explain that Chez Flan only does vegan functions.

A website can perform the same function as a newsletter, with less labour once it is up and running. It is ideal for new *ogoers* who do not yet have offices at their disposal, but do have access to business facilities from time to time. If you're not sure how to go about it, ask around for guidance— there are increasing numbers of computer experts in *ogo* operations.

Telepathy

Most of us do not consider ourselves skilled in extra-sensory perception, and so we ignore psychic messages. Being telepathic is simply being receptive to a particular frequency, much like a satellite dish picking up extra channels. All of us are capable of some telepathy, as the new groundbreaking study by E.J. Smithers has indicated, so if you get a strong urge to go to the Lourdes gallery, as I did last Thursday, rather than to the *Hello, Dolly* opening you had planned on, by all means go. As it turned out on Thursday, the anti-artist Plem was at the gallery to dismiss his work, a retrospective on taupe, and the refreshments were out of this world.

Serendipity

When one doesn't respond to telepathy, serendipity often takes over, and you get to the right place anyway. Perhaps on my way to *Hello, Dolly*, I would have run into Della, who had a tip about Plem from a Westin *hey-you*. Since most of life in one good outfit is unexpected, *ogoers* are usually responsive to serendipity. If one's heart is so set on getting to something that something else is passed up, then expectations have set in, and trouble is sure to be around the corner.

Security and the *ogoer*

Investigating the security field

Security and insecurity are often misconceived as polar opposites. Instead, think of security as a little crease within insecurity, a kick pleat enfolded within the larger flowing fabric of unpredictable life. An *ogoer's* place is on the edge or fold, where she can reinforce feelings of safety for those inside while basking in the insecurity expanse herself. At many events, this border between security and insecurity is physically guarded by security staff, who can make it difficult to enter the fold, so to speak. Employed to shield people from the vast unknown and to keep them safely tucked into their events, security guards continually scan their site for alien elements (i.e., us), having been trained to identify suspicious people as "loose threads or lint on an otherwise clean, pressed garment" (in the words of the *Big Eagle Security* training manual).

Ogoers are also proficient scanners— one must size up each event to see how she'll best fit into it. In most cases an *ogoer* has only moments to scan and adapt, making it necessary for her to have an organized mind as well as a quick eye. The effective *ogoer* has a system roughly comparable to *Big Eagle*'s classification and procedural guidelines. When a *Big Eagle* guard sees someone with "unnatural hair colour and athletic footwear loitering by an exit," for example, they know they have spotted a "class IV individual" who requires "close observation" (*Big Eagle Manual* 223-4). Although *ogo* operations will never be that cut and dried, an *ogoer* must categorize events as she scans them in order to make quick, precise adjustments.

A security index

Many years ago, an *ogoer* would mentally construct her own classification system with whatever criteria came into her head, e.g., size, type of food, dominant hairstyles. Janine Barrille, for instance, swore by her hairstyle index, and would talk and walk one way where curly brown hair prevailed and another where auburn page-boys were the majority. From the beginning of my operations I classified events according to their accessibility, and created an index that was, for a time, useful to many *ogoers*, including Gerry Masooka, although she certainly developed it further. I devised a continuum of types of events depending on how public or private they were. At the inclusive end (#1) are open air music festivals and environmental celebrations. Exclusive extremes (#7) include knightings.

1	2	3	4	5	6	7
music festivals	theatre benefits	church picnics/ lesbian solstice parties	academic functions	business conferences	political campaigns	monarchy events

It seemed to work just fine until Gerry went to a folk festival thinking that a low exclusivity rating ensured low security. Once she got through the gate, which can be taxing even with a ticket, she was foiled at the food tent where she had to pretend to be on the salad crew, and to get lunch had to rip up fifty heads of lettuce. While tearing greens, Gerry came up with this theory: *The most inclusive and the most exclusive events (#1 and #7) have equal, not opposite, levels of security.* It seems that, despite their contrasting appearances, the same amount of control is exerted within events of both categories— by volunteer guards at inclusive, public gatherings, and by a whole range of protocols and security measures at exclusive functions. Following Gerry's realization, my continuum was reconceptualized from a straight line into a horseshoe shape with event types #1 and #7 situated on each tip. People continue to find it helpful.

It is important to realize that although the horseshoe shape is constant, the placement of the various event types is fluid. Academic functions, for instance, have moved from #6 to #4 over the last few years, and seem to be on their way back to at least #5, if the renewed nametag preoccupation at conferences can be taken as an indicator. I have no explanation for this, but

Deirdre claims it is a backlash against popular culture studies. I should also mention combination events, where the security level is always dictated by the lower-rated category. A religious music festival, for instance, is a #1. And finally, there are many event types that resist being fixed in a class at all. Weddings come to mind. These are usually situated between theatre and church events; however, we have all attended some weddings that would be more accurately placed between politics and royalty.

Ratings and operations

Extremes

In general, #1 and # 7 events require *hey-you* support, as inside information is critical. Anything to do with the British monarchy involves some travel, and usually floor plans (perhaps you recall the *ogoer* who ended up in the Queen's chambers during a royal ball of some sort). As well, one's name must appear on a guest list. I confess to having no interest in royal goings-on at all, what with British cooking, and so my information on such events is scant. You might join the Imperial Order of Sisters of Charity who send a representative to the Royal Spring Tea every year. Also in #7 are embassy functions, staged as well in the grand manner, and occasionally featuring royals from here or there. Again, your name must be on a guest list, since people are announced on entering and it is risky to take someone else's name, attendance rates being 90-95% at these events. Embassy security guards are vigilant and get upset by briefcases and purses, so leave these at the hostel or wherever. Every #7 event is studded with guards, uniformed or not, and you must pretend they do not exist. They will consider any notice from you suspicious, as will fellow guests.

Non-professional security staff, who secure at #1 events, must on the other hand get lots of attention. Acknowledge their authority by asking permission for something— e.g., *Is it all right to take pictures?* Volunteer guards, in particular team leaders, may use their temporary posts to experiment with dictatorship. Identifiable by their cell phones and berets, these folks are best distracted by small uprisings which they will be eager to subdue. Although not the most imaginative tactic, a series of minor explosions at the open air *Workers' Music Festival* last year kept security teams well occupied.

Invisible security systems

Events rated in the #2-#3 range do not have designated security people very often, but they do have gatekeepers who take surveillance seriously. Cultural events, with their who's-who focus, tend to be more guarded than #3 functions, although the lesbian potluck I dropped in to last week would be an exception. Gatekeepers rarely stray from doorways and registration tables, but can sometimes be found close to floral displays. As with the volunteer security force, verify a gatekeeper's position of control so she won't feel compelled to do so at your expense. Tell her if someone left their lights on outside, for instance, or ask who did the flowers. At small, stylish functions, gatekeepers will exude distaste if they think you are an outsider, and then they will directly challenge you. To avoid confrontation, I prefer to counter-exude feelings of self-worth and entitlement.

The mother factor

Those of us in our middle years might do well to skim J.J. Mulmer's *The Maternal Bond: Double Agency in Law Enforcement*, which argues that most people take on security roles to resolve issues of maternal authority. To my mind, the book goes too far, but the general premise was proven to me two Wednesdays ago when, innocently, I paid attention to an art opening (#3) gatekeeper by admiring her suit, a slashed taffeta ensemble. She replied, *Like hell you like it! I do not need your approval and who asked you here?* According to Mulmer, professional security guards in #5-#7 events are unlikely to act on their maternal resentments, hoping instead for bomb scares and assassination attempts.

Common ground

Regardless of the type of event, *ogoers* always engage security people rather than avoid them. Remember that security guards and *ogoers* share the border between security and insecurity; although we are facing opposite directions, we are on common ground. Mainly, though, *ogoers* do not hide from security guards, because we are not impostors. Your one good outfit is not a disguise. Rather than pretending to be someone else, an *ogoer* is in a fluid state of amness, where an unfixated self becomes, with the right outfit, infinitely versatile. Amness makes our presence comforting to others, especially those who feel trapped within particular roles and identities.

Collaborative measures

Although *ogoers* are independent operators, many of us work on collaborative ventures, especially if the projects will improve solo operations. Often, group efforts are responses to security crackdowns, which can be so difficult for individual *ogoers* to negotiate. Following the lobster robberies and subsequent security reinforcement at the Edmonton Four Seasons in May '95, for instance, six local *ogoers*, including myself, formed a tactical squad. We went on a suspicious person rotation, taking turns lurking in the lobby in non-good-outfits. Given the assumptions about poor people in relation to criminal behaviour, it took no effort to gain undivided attention from security forces, effectively diverting it from *ogoers* operating in the banquet hall and conference rooms.

Planned ejection

Being a suspicious person on that occasion involved a forced exit, which I have never been keen on. We agreed, though, that the only way to keep guards busy long enough for other *ogoers* to enjoy lunch was to have them eject the suspicious person. Post-ejection arrangements were made with three *hey-*

yous at the Hilton, so each ejectee could think, or in Louise's case, bellow, *'Tis a far far better place that I go!* as she was being escorted out of the Four Seasons. For my ejection, I jogged into the banquet room in Lenore's grey sweat suit. Removal took quite a while, as the Four Seasons guards have had sensitivity training, but it was unpleasant nonetheless. Should you ever be ejected, do as I did, and have your bad outfit take the heat by, quite literally, letting it absorb the hostility and fear of those expelling you. The fabric of your non-good-outfit must be synthetic— non-breathable— so this heat is locked into its surface. This might seem unkind to the clothing, but after all it is the outfit they are responding to, as all that research on maids has proven.

Engagement

Arriving

Now that you know where you are going, and have an idea of what you may find when you get there, it is time to train for the most critical moment in operations— the entrance. The first forty-five seconds you're at an event, like the first twelve hours after an organ transplant, are when rejection is most likely to occur.

The hello, Dolly

The classic entrance for contrasters, the hello, Dolly, begins within view of the registration table. With chest high and head rotated slightly back as if responding to photographers begging for one last shot, glide past the registration desk into the dining room. Strike a here-I-am pose for a four-count, then sweep through room in a continuous curve. Join luminaries if there are any.

The shadow

The shadow is the standard blender entrance. One simply attaches to another person or a group and invisibly enters a function. Join a conversation in the dining-room line-up or, even better, in the women's washroom. For tightly controlled conferences, shadow smokers as they noisily return from smoking outside. The shadow spouse is a great favourite at medical, political, religious and professional sports events where the possibility of one's being Big Bob Johnson's or Reverend Macree's wife explains one's presence very nicely. Simply wait until a real wife goes to the ladies' room and take her place.

The rabbit

Perfect for those with nervous temperaments and no taste for the kind of chit-chat required by the shadow, the rabbit uses quick, jerky movements in a four/four tempo: eight quick half steps, two slow, rest. In a rush with urgent business, the rabbit makes sudden stops to check papers, ask where Room C is, or check the time, then rushes off, dropping kleenex, pens, wallet-inserts with children's pictures. People may be sympathetic, irritated or contemptuous, but they leave rabbits alone.

The searching rabbit mutters *Where is she?* from time to time, leaves messages on the bulletin board by the registration desk (one should always do this anyway), talks into a cell phone, perhaps has someone paged, and continually surveys the room. Good for marketing and sales events and trade shows.

The rabbit easily adapts to different venues. Rush into a concert hall, for instance, with what appears to be a bouquet— layers of white tissue tied over branches or a broom head— and continue right through to backstage. Pick up the pace, as stage managers can be observant, and go over side stage, down the stairs, and into the auditorium to enjoy the event.

The hovercraft

The hovercraft was my sister's specialty, and I'm sure she still excels at it, although it has been some time since I have seen her. For those who have a hard time keeping their feet on the ground, the hovercraft will come naturally, allowing you to float into a room and silently manoeuvre. Use continuous, even steps as you roll from heel to toe on one foot and then the other, and stay conscious of the shoulder area, which must remain level. Hovercrafting is what one does when treading on hot coals— weight is spread so evenly throughout a moving foot that there are no points of contact to get burned. A hovercrafter will look particularly elegant when wearing a flowy skirt or scarf. One should glide slowly, as speeding hovercrafters create a breeze.

Matching entrances with architecture

Although there are countless ways to enter a room, stay with the previous four basic entrances for the first two months of operation. To some extent, interior design and architecture can be your entrance guides. The natural look, for instance, with its exposed pipes, stucco walls and greenery, calls for a grounded walk, feet planted solidly, weight on the heels. The hello, Dolly or the shadow would be fine, either being suitable as well to other styles where high ceilings and exposed beams are featured, e.g., Tudor, colonial, English pub and country house. Futuristic environments with their chrome and sharp, spare lines, require the smooth entrance of the hovercraft, as do Bauhaus structures, Japanese interiors, and other places leaning towards the austere. Contrasting these are the old hotels that are all curves and romance, the one in my centre imitating a Jacobean manor-house. There are tapestries, tassels, pewter, and dark brown books everywhere, and in its main sitting areas, creamy walls and jewel-coloured carpet and upholstery. Using the wavy line of the settee in the foyer as my guide, I meander into the main hall, gazing and loose-limbed. The same approach is appropriate for Victorian, Art Nouveau, and to a lesser extent Art Deco sites. A popular style since the late eighties, Global Fusion is characterized by terra-cotta walls with plaster, brick or stone pillars, cacti, carpets and other textiles in deep earthy colours, and displays of masks, musical instruments, ceramic plates or shells. Use the shadow to attach yourself to an eclectic group.

Environmental adjustments

Once you are inside an event, it is useful to be seen making small adjustments to the environment. Like picking a bit of lint off your jacket or smoothing your scarf, environmental corrections show that you have exacting standards and firm control. Adjusting the thermostat, lights, fan, curtains (choose only one) is effective. You might also have someone paged, and always, as previously mentioned, leave a note on the bulletin board, for example, *Charles and Pat— resv. at Four Seasons, 5:30*. If you are attending a session before lunch, go into the room before anyone else is there to unplug the microphone or overhead projector or to remove the water jug from the speaker's table. As the session begins, smoothly remedy whatever small problem you have created.

Connecting

One should greet someone within thirty seconds of arriving at an event. Do not be too familiar. For most functions, the best approach continues to be generic affability, which includes such standards as, *Wow— you look great, nice to see you again*, or *I thought you might be here*. People over thirty-five are worried about memory loss, so they will return the greeting while trying to remember who you are and will be grateful for cues such as, *It's been a few months*, or, *Well, I'm finally working out again*, and *Gee, there's Carol!* Move on to someone else, or the refreshments, before things get too specific.

Instant intimacy warning

Be careful of instant intimates. Belligerently nice, these people are engaged in some sort of battle, perhaps imaginary, and are conscripting allies. A passionate response to your generic greeting is the first warning sign; a fixed smile, darting eyes and whispered confidences are other signals that you must move on. Break contact carefully. Instant intimates become nasty when they feel betrayed. I am still smarting from a certain sociopathic encounter many years ago. It is perhaps the only *ogo* event that I cannot yet recall without pain.

Circulating

To maximize word power, the wise *ogoer* matches her conversational style to her outfit. People who talk the way they dress, as if their words are part of them, appear to be seamless and therefore trustworthy. Classic, fitted outfits call for refined speech, which is typified by

1) clipped *t*'s
2) select adjectives, and
3) highly versatile pronouncements

An example for a performance event might be, *Thought it was excellent, really, quite excellent, savage use of light.* (Note: Don't overdo Britishisms such as "savage," "bloody" and "wretched," even at theatre events, as they put people on guard.) Draped and unstructured clothing goes with flowing sentences punctuated by short sighs and ending with a question. To complement the combination look many of us favour— loose jacket over fitted dress— use sweeping gestures and refined statements or, should your hands be engaged with food, syntactically mix a declaration or two with questions. *Absolutely fine event. Did you notice the German book display? Particularly enjoyed the closing speaker.*

Timing

There is rhythm to every verbal exchange, just as there is texture to every wearable, and you must know when to pick up a thread of conversation, and especially when to drop it. The easiest conversations are with one other person who dominates, requiring you only to maintain timing with regular *Uh-huhs* and *Isn't-that-somethings?* Eye contact is your best guide, with blinking often providing beats. Never pause more than three blinks, even if someone has something in their eye.

Brevity is important, unless more than three people are involved, and then the object is to contribute and leave, adding *Hmmms* and flat declamations (*I don't believe it. Who would have thought?*) until there's a brief pause and the others are looking at you. Open with, *Isn't that interesting?* and move into, *Do you think that new book by Dirshey could apply?*

Keynotes

Every group, occupational or social, has its buzzwords and acronyms, and by dropping one or two into conversation you'll get in sync with whatever's going on. If you are at a conference, check the program and you will see the right word repeated in several session titles, and in the welcoming address. You might also mingle outside with the smokers, who, banned from the main action, will assert themselves with emphatic, repeated use of in-words. At family and social functions, linger in the women's washroom to find out who's newsworthy and return to the group with simple lines like *Too bad about Delores*, or *Great that Bob's back on track.*

Playing the part

The masterful *ogoer* knows how to be a conversational back-up to someone else's solo, to in effect give something and move on before the recipient has had a chance to reciprocate. Aside from giving someone full range of expression, this "gift" creates a subtle state of indebtedness in the speaker, making you, in turn, more secure at the event. Depending on the size and duration of the function you are attending, there should be between one and five people who feel vaguely grateful to you (rather than clearly grateful, which so quickly becomes resentment).

Conversational hazards

There are times when we all get stuck for something to say. At these moments, a repertoire of versatile phrases is terribly handy, and you'd do well to think of two or three right now. The go-anywhere statement is brief, musing, and if it is to sound sincere, should be delivered with a certain melancholy.

> *It always comes back to that, doesn't it.*
> *Momentum seems to be the issue, all right.*
> *Everything's relative, as per usual.*

The other conversation hazard is becoming attached to your conversee— being unable to stop as the conversation intensifies and heat builds in your chest and throat. Such fiery moments can allow an *ogoer* to forget her primary purpose, and it is again a fine idea to have a few lines memorized— this time for distancing.

> *Oh, there's Wanda! What a great outfit.*
> *My feet are killing me.*
> *Well, there's a reason for everything.*

Of course there is the bigger issue of forming attachments at events and how they affect operations. Longing can be activated during a conversation and for some of us can get out of hand very quickly. This is not the place for scientific detail, but I do want to mention the new findings on fleeps, those microscopic burrs which are released from bone marrow under certain vibratory conditions. Encoded with our deepest needs, fleeps are activated when the voice of another person vibrates our clavicles. This person then absorbs our fleeps and we may well absorb hers or his. And so, although the conversation may be about baseball or Cher, intimate information is exchanged and a bond is formed. (For a more thorough explanation, see *The Big Fleep* by NymNym Peters.) Only last week I was chatting with a dentistry student about washing silk and soon we were talking about wearing it, then not wearing it, and so forth. As my protein requirements for the day had been met, I wholeheartedly fleeped. If you are not well nourished, or are unsure about breakfast, do be prudent. Stock up on crackers and cheese, or arrest the fleep exchange by drinking something acidic.

Posture

All too much is made of body language. Rather than worrying about what every finger, toe and facial feature is doing, think of your body as three main centres: head, heart and groin. Depending on the nature of the event, you want to extend one of these centres. The heart or chest area is expanded for most family/church and evening social events. It is collapsed for any academic function, where head and pelvis dominate, and one uses pelvic-referral gestures (belt-adjusting) while at the same time thrusting the chin forward as far as the neck will allow. (Rose Ouelett, a veteran *ogoer* with an academic specialty, always straps a rock to her sternum before giving a conference paper.) It is the pelvis that is forward at sports, medical and political events, enhanced further with hands in pockets, a wide stance, or thigh tapping. If you can't decide what should be sticking out, do the wave: rolling head forward, then chest, then groin, in a very slow, fluid movement, so as not to disturb anyone. This technique was perfected in Ottawa, where a great many functions are difficult to categorize. Sandra and Carmel, veterans in that city, say the wave is most effective when done on a steady count of twelve (four beats per centre). Faster undulations can be misunderstood, as Penny Dodds discovered, awkwardly, at the Girl Guides of Canada leadership rally and brunch.

Accessories can accentuate the protruding centre, and if you frequent pelvic events you might consider a belt with emphatic buckle. For those of us who cover a range of functions, scarves are the most versatile, as they can move from pelvis to chest to head as belt, neckpiece or turban (see Cross-functional coordinates).

Reassurance

As the Oscar-nominated documentary *Naked Pretender* shows, people everywhere, especially important ones, are afraid of being found out. It is important to reassure people that their disguise is working so they won't question yours. More important, they will want you to stay. Reassurance is the *ogoer's* offering— as long as people are hungry for it, we will continue to eat well. The critical thing is timing. It takes a good sense of rhythm to know exactly when to say something, but don't despair if you have always been offbeat. Watch the veteran *ogoers* in your centre and eventually you'll catch on. Knowing what to say is comparatively easy, as, one way or the other, people will tell you what they want to hear. Listen for variations of what Phoebe calls the "big three"— our three primary worries in the western hemisphere: Am I competent, Am I loveable, When will I die.

Advice exchanges

Advice giving is considered excessive, something like sending a crate of chocolate when a card will do, but I confess to giving it from time to time. When someone clearly wants to hear something and you are standing right there, perhaps feeling a little alone in the world, it is hard to resist complying. People are very close and grateful to you when you convince them to go ahead and do something they know they shouldn't. Last spring, at the Canadian Construction Association banquet, I leaned over the table to say, *Of course you must, you absolutely must,* to two beautiful pipefitters who wanted to abandon work and bike ride around the world. We spent a warm romantic evening over more wine, eventually walking through the river valley talking and kissing.

It is common practice, on the other hand, to ask for advice, as that is the most effective means of reassuring people in authoritative roles. Just this morning, over croissants and juice at the Ambulatory Pediatrics Symposium, I asked a morose psychiatrist about facial tics. Another popular form of reassurance among non-*ogoers* and *ogoers* alike includes inventing data. At the Latex Futures conference last week, I was able to explain to a concerned parent the high correlation between low test scores in junior high science and high commercial achievement in later life. I am selective about who I reassure, as one can easily become drained, especially if the reassured person is unable to reciprocate with any kind of warmth or humour. I avoid, for instance, willfully impassive people unless they are gatekeepers who must be appeased. Identifiable by their scraping laughs, these people need to be reassured that they are in control, but it takes a good deal of energy to establish eye contact and get them focused, and then a good deal more to think of something reassuring to say.

Ghostwear

The people who are potentially most damaging to *ogoers* are those who are most difficult to reassure. According to Deirdre's prevalence study, 2% of people are reassurance-resistant. For whatever reason, they recoil from their own longings, retreating to their marrow in a state of I-am-notness. Their poor outfits are abandoned, forced to fend for themselves with bare bones support. Commonly known as ghostwear, the outfit will have a molded quality, with non-absorbent fabric, and a sheen that sometimes defies its texture. The face of the disappeared person is heavily outlined, i.e., with lipliner, eyeliner, and highlighter, and has a scotch-guarded look, although as Shirley says, we all have our waxy days. Jewellery is inevitably metallic. (A ghost-wearing group in Oxford, actually distributes their own line of stainless steel pendants, chokers, and eyeglass frames.) Your *ogo* will react immediately to ghostwear, especially if it has aban-donment issues, and will probably cling to you. (A cling-free slip is generally a good idea.) At the genetic mutation thing in Seattle a few years back, Marlena didn't realize she was talking to ghostwear until she was shrinkwrapped by her Chanel knit dress and the ghostwear called security. Marlena had to take such itty bitty steps— her *ogo* is calf-length— that I resorted to the fire alarm so she'd have enough time to get away.

Counter-reassurance

An *ogoer* will sense the essential absence in ghostwear and may
be inclined to reassure them that such emptiness is part of life
and so on. This would be incorrect. Ghostwear wants to feel
complete and completely in control, to be reassured, in other
words, that there is no emptiness. It's best to offer them flaws
to expose. Avoid obvious things like food bits on one's lapel,
and begin with an arrogant stance (chin and chest forward).
Interrupt their conversation to display ignorance of the topic at
hand and hint, in spite of yourself, at a failed marriage or
gambling problem. Register pain when your flaw is exposed.
Slowly deflate, as if you suddenly understand the smallness of
your being, shuffle away without looking up, and you should
be safe for the remainder of the event.

Layered flaws

A slight deviation from the ghostwear strategy is used for those
occupationally suspicious people whose livelihoods depend on
falsehood— accountants, beauticians and the clergy, for example. Once again, the layered approach is best, with one or two
faux pas leading to a primary lie. Dependable primary lies
include the following: one's happiness, one's satisfaction with
spouse or children, one's belief in God, interest in meditation,
and so forth (just listen in on other conversations around the
cheese trays if you're unsure). Don't go overboard. I simply say

"I haven't eaten a thing all day" while reaching for the biggest sausage roll on the platter. To reassure the occupationally suspicious of their skills in detection, you musn't be obvious. A quick look away from their scrutinizing eyes, a flush if you can do that on demand, a nervous hand-through-hair gesture or facial twitches— *one* of these will be sufficient.

Loss protection

Disagreeable strangers

It's an odd thing when people dislike you, but it happens to everybody, and I suppose one shouldn't spend too much time wondering why. Without knowing you, without talking to you, even, they dislike you. I am, this moment, sitting in a coffee shop where the waitress dislikes me. She greets people cheerfully but glares at me, clunks my coffee down so it spills onto the saucer and a minute later slides my butter pat across the counter right into my elbow. To the man next to me she says, *There you go, darling,* and places his cappuccino down ever so carefully.

Of course, when someone behaves badly, one should say, *Well, that's their problem.* From time to time, though, miserable people jeopardize operations and one needs to be prepared with more than a catchphrase. I learned this rather late in my operations, only months ago, in fact, at an Opiate Dependency Program conference. Lunch began with a raging young doctor from the inner city health unit spilling tea on me. I was worried about my jacket and shoes, as you can imagine, but instead of apologizing, she said something sarcastic. Indignation got the better of me. The next day I was still conspicuously irritated, and blending was difficult. It wasn't until suppertime that day, while leaning against one of the faux marble pillars in the entry to our new downtown shopping complex, that I knew what to do. I borrowed a pen from a clerk in the Belgian chocolate shop, then discreetly documented the incident on the pillar. The relief was instantaneous and I was soon enjoying a stress-free supper.

Ever since that experience I have documented affronts on the pillar. To describe an event is to control it, and I generally regain self-assurance after writing two or three lines about an unpleasant incident. Because it is so efficient, many other *ogoers* have adopted this practice. Known now as the "irritation totem," the pillar holds many tiny stories, such as, *forced to polka at Policeman's Ball* and *served cold coffee at Lindsey Spinelli's graduation,* as well as several longer narratives.

Hostile acquaintances

Sometimes one runs into someone who has a reason for their hostility towards you. Many of you will remember Dorothy Major's time as hostel manager, and some of you know I had a role in abbreviating it. There she was at the Healthy Communities convention last spring, speaking to a security person and gesturing in my direction as I was about to dig into the low fat mandarin chicken stir fry. One must have their wits about them in these instances. I went straight up to Dorothy and said, *Hello, lovely to see you doing so well, won't you please join us, so good to see you out and about*, and so on, maintaining eye contact except to share a quick understanding smile with the security person. Depending on where you are in your lunch, and how good it is, this type of intervention is worth the effort. The only alternative is to slink away.

Volunteerism: the everlasting nay

When your reassurance goes a little overboard— and it happens to all of us, so don't feel badly— people do not want to let you go. They invite you into their lives, sometimes as an intimate friend, sometimes as a board member. Sex is one thing, but volunteerism is quite another and must be refused. Run screaming from any volunteer "opportunities" involving childcare, food preparation, and mail-outs. No matter how promising something sounds, take time to think it over, as over-eagerness is never elegant. I would hate to think of anyone else gushing, *Yes, I'd love to, oh thank you!* as I once did, only to spend an evening stuffing envelopes in a basement room with three angry teenagers and a bag of nachos. You might, however, thoughtfully consider board membership for organizations with supper or breakfast meetings, these being the more difficult meals. Even then, be selective, as board meetings and good food rarely coincide.

Group invention: becoming a society

If you deeply, chronically, long to belong to a group, consider inventing your own association or society. This can also be an excellent way to secure tickets to cultural events, to express an opinion through the media, and to gain support (in its various forms) from government and corporations. I frequently become the Japanese Business Association, and am regularly dined by the provincial forestry minister. Several other virtual corporations, such as Pat Yulski's Universal Retrieval Corp. and Jan Ferby's GenDar Plastics, also benefit from the hospitality budgets of certain elected officials. Over one fine meal, Jan, Pat and I created the Society to Protect Love in Families, or SPLIF. SPLIF attracted a fine group of relaxed people to its board of directors, and garnered from several ministries a healthy fund, which we have been able to redistribute.

Becoming an official group is as simple as choosing a name and, if you have access to print resources, nice letterhead and business cards. You can be as many groups as you like, but it is a good idea to use one continually so it gets a strong profile. Check names of current associations before settling on yours. You will be surprised at what's already out there, and by how touchy other groups get when a new one comes along with a name similar to theirs.

At the table

Food and fear

People are afraid to eat. Once the stomach gets attention, all sorts of other hungers demand to be fed and there you sit, transparent as fine crystal. It is also frightening to witness the appetites of others, to watch a stranger flush as a dollop of butter drops onto a baked potato or quiver with a mouthful of chocolate mousse. If not for table manners, primal urges would overflow onto everything.

Aside from being useful implements, cutlery and glassware keep us well occupied at most tables and can be discreetly clenched, stroked, and licked as one's urges require. If emotions are percolating too close to the surface, distract yourself with protocol. Engage a tablemate by asking something along the lines of, *Do you by chance remember who that writer was who just died?* At informal meals offer someone the basket of buns. If, on the other hand, you want to indicate that your passions are in no need of restraint, use cutlery and manners with fearless ease. When it is more appropriate to show that you are barely under control, clank things against each other. For instance, one clanks at the power meals of sales conventions, where all interactions, including those with food, are competitive, and one wields fork and knife to spear, then shred, everything on one's plate.

Formal dining

Daunting though a formal meal may appear, there is really not much you have to know. Approach the table— usually it is rectangular— with regal bearing, and another person will pull your chair out for you. Except for a quick glance to check the chair position, gaze upward as you slowly sit with spine erect. During the meal, progress from the outside in with cutlery and from the inside out with glasses. That's really all there is to it, aside from smoothing your napkin onto your lap without looking at it, and using your knife in continental rather than American fashion. The old practice of leaving something on your plate is now passé, but on the other extreme, exuberant eating is still considered venal. Of course, at some contemporary tables, venality has its place— I am thinking of the 1992 BITE fest— but in my experience, these are not formal affairs.

Until recently, at a formal meal one never spoke about personal experience, including one's enjoyment of the food itself. I learned this the hard way, when, in my first *ogo* year, at the Dusseldorf Heritage Society brunch, I said I adore potatoes. A great deal of throat clearing and napkin patting went on among my tablemates and when they did resume eye contact it was with a murky tolerance that recalled my grade two teacher, Sister Nedley Marie. For many years, I did not again divulge my tastes, and learned to discuss art-for-all initiatives, capital gains tax, and celebrities. The new formality now permits personal observations but continues to forbid personal responses. One must therefore react with a detached, *Ah, well then,* or *Yes, of course,* when someone tells you they dream about lice, or that yams soften their stool. In terms of who-to-talk-to protocol, speak to the person on your right for ten minutes or so, then the person on your left. If your tablemates don't know this rule, and those on either side of you are both turned away, look meaningfully into the distance, then slowly around the table, smiling supportively at whoever meets your gaze.

Informal meals

Informal meals are by far the most prevalent, outnumbering formal functions by six to one in most *ogo* operations. The hallmark of informal dining is the round table with family-style seating. Eight to twelve people share each table and pass around the bread basket, salt and pepper and butter. One must appear to be natural and relaxed and should talk of pleasant things like cats and Irish music. Tensions at these meals invariably rise when familial overtones activate family memories, and are apt to become heightened if meatballs, apple crisp or other homestyle cooking appears. I am thinking of the annual Boilermakers' Union supper last March. My tablemates were happily teasing each other about hair loss until a big pot of stew was plunked down and one of them took the ladle. After a shaky silent moment, they began squabbling: How come he gets to go first, you're taking all the meat, you're not the boss of us, etc. When this kind of behaviour erupts, do avoid triggering maternal associations. Do not comment on what people leave on their plate, do not thrust your chest forward, particularly if you have large breasts, and do not stack your dishes into a neat little pile once you have finished eating. Unresolved breastfeeding issues abound in any group, as well as resentments about school lunches, birthday cakes, tuna casseroles and who knows what else. Once you remind someone of their mother, they blame you for the whole ball of wax, and enjoyable dining becomes impossible.

Entering a meal in progress

When a meal is in progress one must know where one is going. There are usually empty chairs at the tables farthest away from the food, so rush in that direction if you have no other plan. Talk into a cell phone as you go, ask those at the table *Can I join you?* then put the phone away with a wistful, *It never stops, does it.*

The reserved sign

Although we sometimes have to bolt in and hope for the best, seasoned *ogoers* prepare for many meals with a Reserved sign.

Conveniently generic— I have only ever seen one type of Reserved sign— it is primarily used in two ways. For crowded, self-conscious functions, choose a fairly central table where all the chairs except two or three have been angled to signify "taken." Place the Reserved sign, busy yourself with the conference folder or your daytimer, and when the people return, usually together, say, *Oh I'm sorry, I was told this was Dr. Tegler's table. They must have made a mistake.* There will be consternation, someone will notice the Reserved sign, and you can then reassure them that Dr. Tegler is always late anyway, no need to worry, and so on. Describe him so they can keep a look-out while you get food, and once re-seated, discreetly scan the room as you chew. When your tablemates feel they might be taking someone's place, especially someone important, they will not challenge your right to be there.

The second strategy involves placing the Reserved sign on a table mid-morning while everyone else is in session, clearing the salt and pepper, etc., to the side so that the sign is very visible. At lunch sit close to the reserved table, and join your tablemates in wondering who could be sitting there. When the table remains empty, join your tablemates in wondering why they didn't show up and how they could be so inconsiderate. A little righteousness creates a nice bond among people, and once again, your place at the table will be secured.

Receptions and other unseated functions

If it is a cocktail party and reception kind of thing, never actually stop at the food trays. Instead, slowly pass them, each time plucking off a delicacy. Continue a slow, spiral walk through the room, and don't alter your pace as you approach the food. Standing functions have a slow, continuous rhythm, and sudden stops or quick movements are disruptive. Think of skating.

At receptions, people stand in semi-circles of three to five people which slowly break up and re-form every nine to thirteen minutes. It is best to stand in the middle of these groups and glide from one to the other without looking around. Go for food every third to fourth re-formation, circling back into a newly formed group as you chew.

Nutrition

Quality control

The fully operational *ogoer* enjoys a balanced diet, but not without taking certain measures. There is first of all the issue of mass feedings at large events, which are the source of one third to one half of the average *ogoer's* meals. Even the best kitchens tend to overcook when dealing with huge amounts of food, but most institutions do offer alternative vegetarian meals. Not only are these dishes made in much smaller batches than regular fare, but they are made with far more care, as many chefs still consider vegetarians to be picky and troublesome. You can ask for the vegetarian meal once you are seated and the waiter is plunking salads down, but pre-ordering is a good idea as it will establish your place at the event. Go to the dining room about 10:30 a.m. when waiters will be setting up tables, ask the most earnest of them to check your order, and point to the table you will be seated at during lunch. Use your Reserved sign to secure the table (refer to Functional accessories). Should anyone doubt your rightful place at lunch, they will relax when the waiter seeks you out with a special order. I recently experienced this at the Natural Health convention, where I had joined a table of shamanic plastic surgeons for lunch. An insular group, they bristled and sighed until I signalled the waiter and he brought my soy-free veggie burger with extra cheese. Curiosity seemed to replace their suspicion, and as they tucked into tofu scramble, we chatted nicely about dairy products. (As all meals at this event were vegetarian, I had to do a little investigating before making my special order.)

The dark leafy green challenge

Dark leafy greens (*dlgs*) are another concern for the *ogoer*. Except for the occasional spinach dip at baby showers and spanokapita at Greek weddings, it is difficult to find this valuable source of iron and magnesium. If you have advance notice about an event, you might call the host kitchen on behalf of event organizers to request Swiss chard, for instance, as the side vegetable, but cooks often refuse to cooperate, since *dlgs* get limp, cold and tasteless so quickly. After much planning and effort, we remedied the problem in this particular urban centre with a multi-prong approach. Articles on *dlgs* were placed in *Cutting Edge Cuisine* and other influential gourmet publications, a conference on hydroponics and other advanced growing techniques was offered to *dlg* growers, a Popeye retrospective was held in two major theatres, a line of evening wear designed on a *dlg* theme was launched, and so on. It was an exhaustive campaign, involving the most skilled *hey-yous* and *ogoers*, and it has paid off. Bok Choy Surprise is now a staple at the Four Seasons lunch buffet, and spinach has completely replaced iceberg lettuce in the house salads at two other hotels.

Surplus consumption

For those of us who launch operations on an empty stomach, overeating in the initial phase is common, and shows good survival instincts. After three weeks, though, new *ogoers* should be slowing down, having developed with their confidence the assurance that there will always be plenty to eat. If not, the best approach is to happily continue excessive eating, tasting and chewing with attentive joy. Generally, overeating *ogoers* are correcting long-term nutritional deficiencies, and the more food is appreciated, the more generously will it release nutrients. Conversely, malabsorption of vitamins and low energy are the common result of unhappy eating, examples of which you will see at every table you join.

Turnarounds

There are times when an *ogoer* feels like having the food come to her rather than going out to the food. Those of us in hostels and similar accommodations can capitalize on current tastes for urban grit to make this happen. In my hostel, Trisha Barnes began hosting "Out of the Gutter" literary salons, and they are hugely popular. Guests come with excellent food, and after five or six of us read gritty poetry, everyone sits down to a lovely meal. There was initially consternation about writing the poetry, but Doris, a former English professor, convinced us not to worry so we haven't and it's been fine. Last week we read the list of ingredients from Kraft Dinner and no-name alphabet soup and next week we'll silently stand as an egg timer clicks.

Lingering

Once you have enjoyed a good meal as an *ogoer* you are fully operational. Do linger at the table after dessert so you can savour this accomplishment. Silently congratulate your *ogo* and allow your full belly to press against it in appreciation. Remove crumbs and food particles and if necessary go to the washroom to sponge off spots. An *ogo* needs to know you will still be attentive after it has helped you get a meal. Otherwise it may feel taken for granted and could sabotage future operations. My outfit likes to have its hem stroked, so after dinner, I gently pull the fabric of my skirt hem between the thumb and index finger of the other hand. Every outfit has its individual preferences of course: Marian Shoreline's pantsuit likes to be firmly brushed with a lint remover at the end of every day, and Diana Cardinal's dress prefers reiki. Do learn what your outfit likes and ensure that every piece receives equal attention.

PART III: *OGO* ENERGY

Ogo energy

Making new connections

By now you have enjoyed a good many meals and are feeling well nourished and pleased with yourself. And so you should. You have mastered the mechanics of *ogo* operations, the nuts-and-bolts, bread-and-butter, ground-level basics that must be understood to get things up and running. As you may have sensed, beneath the operational surface there is a lot going on— a whole system of invisible wiring that keeps us energized and interconnected. An understanding of *ogo* energetics increases one's operational capacity, despite conflicting claims by Cecile Wendo, who calls the study of energetics "pernicious anti-materialism" in her book *Ogoing Unplugged*. However, Cecile not only ignores ancient *ogo* principles, she also fails to mention that her *ogoing* twin Chloe, who has a motivational speaker specialty, opens every speech by shouting, *The currency of tomorrow is energy! What's* your *exchange rate?*

The effects of learning about energy are not entirely comfortable, for one typically goes through a rewiring stage that includes loneliness, futility, boredom, irritation, and after a few months, perhaps madness. Some of these states are regionally specific: Manitoban *ogoers* tend towards acute irritability, for instance, and *ogoers* in Kansas are piloting an anti-futile initiative to hopefully manage the endemic indifference among their transitioning sisters. Whatever your location, however, you can expect to feel miserable for a few weeks following your first *ogo* anniversary (83% of *ogoers* experience transitional discomfort thirteen months after their first *ogo* meal; an additional 9% have later onset, at eighteen months). For those of you who had homes, perhaps you once tried to clean out kitchen cupboards and remember that despairing point-of-no-return when everything was spread all over in a huge mess. When one's energy field becomes activated, all other internal systems must be re-ordered, and depending on how much is crammed into one's being, things can be quite messy for a while.

Unpleasant though misery is, it is a sign that one's energetic system is being activated and dormant circuits are being cleared. Eventually one senses a new internal spaciousness. This is the mature stage of *ogoing*, where one has the capacity to be fully operational on both energetic and material levels. It is here that our objectives— liberty, peace, and elegant dining for all— can be wholly contemplated.

Adjustments

Boredom

Boredom is a damp, heavy, unavoidable state of being. *Ogoers* must make peace with it. Sooner or later one has to sit though a conference session, a board meeting, a political speech, where every molecule of one's being silently cries, *Get me out of here or I shall die.* Some people try to make mental lists when bored, or glean fashion tips from other participants, but this skirts the central issue of nothingness. When one is bored, there is nothing but the passage of time to notice, and no way to avoid awareness of one's own temporality and emptiness, although we all try. The speaker is avoiding her nothingness by boring the hell out of everyone, and we avoid it by being irritated with the boredom. In general, Buddhism has a few tips on handling boredom, but see also Shirley Lipshey's *Bored No More.*

Ennui

Some days my heart is not in this. For solace, I go to the Seven Suns Hotel to sit in their indoor courtyard and listen to the little waterfall. My favourite seat is in an alcove which faces rocks and plants and the trickling water from hidden pipes. Through leaves I can see people coming and going from the ballrooms, both set for lunch, which I would love to eat but truly am too tired to do.

Two waiters go by, carrying celery. A porter passes with an empty luggage rack. I continue to sit.

Madness

Madness is improved by earnest planning and accessorizing. It is different for everyone, of course, and is sometimes so subtle it blends nicely into day-to-day life. For others (Petra comes to mind) it arrives in full splendour, complete with hallucinations. According to Michele Duzzen's groundbreaking work, *Mad in Pursuit, but Possessed? No!,* madness is a transitional state where one's receptors and transmitters are not yet synchronized with one's energy field, leaving one's poor aura to lurch around with no neurological support. The nervous system tries madly to catch up, and usually does within three weeks, but until then, one feels rather at loose ends. Michele estimates that approximately 80% of Canadian *ogoers* go mad for an average of nineteen days. (The average is slightly higher in the United States (84%) with a shorter duration of seventeen days, and surprisingly low in Ireland— 72% with an average of eight days.)

Ogoers usually go mad within the first year of operations, often just when they're getting comfortable with things. It is a necessary reformatting stage, the step between that life and this one, between the predictable and the possible. Those of us who have very set ideas about how things should go seem to be mad for a little longer than someone like Shirley, who was quite open-minded even when she ran that investment firm. Madness does not have to be noticeable, as people happily misinterpret one's expression of continual surprise as interest in themselves.

Choosing a time and place

January is a slow conference month, and if you can plan your madness, this would be the time. It is January 15th today, and I am sitting in the vast empty conference floor of the Radisson with sunlight refracting off chrome fixtures and a nice rumbly hum that could be the sound of the universe if it wasn't the ventilation system. There are footstep sounds long before people appear from the hallway, and then they silently go by on the rug, as if we're all underwater. I am sorry my madness is over. This would be the perfect setting.

Managing side effects

When one is mad, things appear unfamiliar and infinite. Time and space don't seem to hold things together any more, and there are intense moments when everything is everything all at once. Nausea is common but can be alleviated. Just as one doesn't look down when walking up a broken escalator or sky diving, a mad person feels less queasy if she focuses on something small and stable. Plan to have a nice big daytimer or crossword puzzle to fill out during this period, find soothing locations like the courtyard previously mentioned, or simply go somewhere pleasant in your mind. I used to imagine myself in a bathtub, with the shower curtain pulled and toiletries nicely arranged on a floating tray, while in the rest of the house, major renovations were underway.

Madness variety

Madness comes in different shapes and sizes, of course, sometimes complicating operations, sometimes enhancing them. Lory-Anne, for instance, saw animals pop out of people's chests, and it was the handiest thing to know who was a buzzard, a lamb, and so forth. Shirley saw windows shatter and go back together as she walked down the street, and I just lost my memory, so everything looked brand new. I must say, once I got used to it, the constant state of discovery was enervating.

Recovery

I knew my madness was over when I took a big breath one morning and the air shot through my body like a breeze through a stuffy room. All that day my body ventilated itself, and I realized that my rib cage was now unlocked, leaving a sense of internal space that felt vast and warm as a summer sky. This space, I would later learn, was my "sun room," the energy centre of the solar plexus. I had become internally powered.

The length of the recovery period depends on the duration of the madness. It is a little like accruing holiday time, with approximately one recovery day for every four mad days. Recovery is an expanded state in which one's senses and skills are heightened and one's capacity for joy is everpresent. There is newfound comfort in the silences and gaps that punctuate one's day, and the compulsion to rush ahead is gone. Frown lines, outfit wrinkles, and operational snags all smooth out and everything seems effortless.

When her recovery time is over, an *ogoer* comes down to earth, in a manner of speaking, and engages once more with the challenges of everyday life. Lory-Anne once again focused on people's faces instead of their animal counterparts and could have conversations without the primal terror that comes when faced with a viper or polar bear. She could still sense certain animals but she could also, finally, stand her ground. (A post-mad *ogoer* never returns to the pre-mad stage. Like Lory-Anne, the post-mad *ogoer* has sturdy I-amness and will be able to look upon anything without being shaken.)

Ogo history

Three periods

Ogoers often yearn for knowledge of their *ogoer* forebears, for some sense of connection to ancestral roots. Some fine research has been documented by *ogoers* recently, including Vera Smyth's *Still Good as New* and L. Klassen's *A Stitch in Time: Recovering Early Ogoers,* a lucid investigation that gives overdue credit to Freda and Jane Salvalaggio in Rio Caliente.

Ogo history has three distinct periods: first, second, and third. Until 1984, all that was known of the first period came from the mystic writings of Shmyx, who so movingly described the *vashli,* an *ogo* presentation ceremony performed by Blaridians in the eighth century BC. (On her fourteenth birthday, a young woman would be presented with an *ogo* by her oldest aunt who had envisioned it during a month of feasting.) On June 7, 1984, the scrolls of Phylo were unearthed in Corinth, bringing the first period to life, and new life to our current period, as we will soon discuss.

The second period began in Oban, Scotland, with the formation of the Sacred Sisters of the Cloth in 1122. The Sacred Sisters pioneered the basic black dress. Cloistered and anonymous in appearance, they didn't explore the versatility of their outfits, but they did much to make the black dress a universal symbol of elegance. Within their convent's woollen mill they also established high weaving standards for Scottish woollens. The second period clearly ended when the convent disbanded and closed the mill on February 12, 1683, to defy an anti-Covenanter group's demand for blankets. (Lady Griselda Baillie, a close aquaintance of the convent's Mother Superior Ignatius, was likely influential in this decision. Joanna Baillie, Lady Griselda's niece, would in later years become literary advisor to a small group of *ogoers* in Inverness; they published a verse anthology in 1823. For more on the covenanters, read J.D. Mackie's *A History of Scotland* [Penguin, Suffolk, 1984]; consult the Orlando Project database for further details on the fascinating Baillies.)

In period three, *ogos* went out of the convent into the convention. Scant records make it difficult to know what conventions *ogoers* first attended, but the Friends of Scarlatti Convention in Rome, September, 1719, and the International Cartography Conference in Barcelona, June, 1720, appear to have been among them. *Ogoers* were soon attending a wide range of functions, including coronation parties and other grand affairs until the *ogo* achieved its current ready-to-wear-anywhere status. Versatility has been the hallmark of period three and will likely continue to preoccupy the next two generations of *ogoers* if the glut of guides on cross-functional coordinating and Francine Lipp's *The Shift Paradigm*, a celebrated new volume on A-line dresses, can be taken as trend indicators.

While the focus on versatility continues, we can also see what's around the corner for fourth period *ogoing*. Many veteran *ogoers*, myself included, are convinced that we are gradually moving away from a material modality into an energetic one. Our own experiences inform this view, but we have also been inspired by Phylonian artifacts and by research.

Energized shopping

The power centre and fashion capital of the Mediterranean, Phylo had the earliest known women's wear markets. Open every Thursday and Saturday from 9:00 a.m. until 7:00 p.m., these markets were designed to facilitate the flow of energy. Phylonians understood something we are only now beginning to realize, that two prime energy currents charge everything— one which stabilizes and another which integrates. The stabilizing force is dense, vibrates at a low frequency, and spirals downward, while the integrating force has a high frequency and moves outward and up. Phylonian markets provided shoppers with a bi-weekly opportunity to rebalance and recharge their energies. (At least we still have the shopping impulse, although the wires became tragically crossed somewhere, so charging only occurs now with credit cards, depleting rather than energizing shoppers. See Levan Hoksham, *No Charge: The Disconnection of Energy and Value in Contemporary Commerce*.) In Phylo, a typical women's wear market would have been laid out as follows:

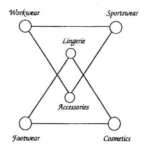

A typical women's wear market in Phylo

The earth was at that time considered a sacred generator, and the shape for best containing its energy on ground level was known to be the triangle. (Homer's famous line "All was divided into three" was likely taken from a Phylonian market day flyer, as his cousin lived in the vicinity.) For a really energizing experience, Phylonians intersected two triangles, and cordoned off the area of overlap so people could privately enjoy highly charged moments.

The path of Phylo

Phylonian women would always start at footwear and proceed across the lower triangle to cosmetics and up to lingerie. As these are foundation products they have strong stabilizing emissions, and Phylonians would feel grounded as they walked this path.

From lingerie, women would move up to sportswear, across to workwear, and back down to accessories, these three products having coordination and integration functions. Typically there was a refreshment stand outside of workwear so shoppers could mingle before visiting the final department.

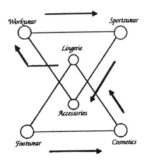

The shopping path of Phylonian women

The charged change area

Note the diamond-shaped intersecting area of the triangles. This is the change area, where stabilizing and integrating energies combined to create a highly charged vortex. Encircling the change areas were limpon trees, as the bangle-shaped limpon leaves buffered energy and provided a charming screen for those inside. When a Phylonian tried on a stabilizing garment, it would amplify her own stability force, giving her the strength to, for instance, train for an endurance sporting event. A woman tried on integrating items to enhance her interactive skills, perhaps to help her resolve a conflict with peers or business associates. You may have noted that lingerie and accessories are on either side of the change area, the power points of the change area. When a woman required high-voltage vision— for a prophecy, for example— she would try on these items. Moments of great illumination occurred in the change area, as you can imagine.

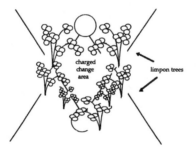

The charged change area

Your circuitry

The point of joints

Look once more at the previous illustrations and note a resemblance between the market plan and the *ogoer* hieroglyphs discovered in Tuscany some years ago.

Tuscany hieroglyphs

It appears that the ancients got their market designs from the human form, somehow knowing that humans were energy conductors. As Bunny Valemore explains in her two-volume set *Posture Takes Its Toll* and *Rebuild Your Bridges in Fourteen Days*, sportswear and workwear correspond to shoulder joints, forming an "integration bridge" from one shoulder to the other.

144

When one slumps her shoulders, or caves in her chest or sticks it out, the integration bridge is closed, according to Valemore, and interactions become strained. Footwear and cosmetics correspond to hip joints, forming a "stability bridge" across the pelvis. Uneven hips or a tilted pelvis destabilize one by cutting off energy flow across the bridge. With the new energy sensors being developed in Fort McMurray, one will soon be able to get her bridges gauged, but until then, use a full length mirror in a dressing room to examine your posture.

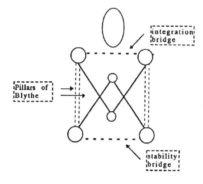

The human energy body

The Pillars of Blythe

Valemore's student Sally Tripp did additional work on the vertical relationship between shoulder and hip joints. She claims, convincingly, that the sportswear shoulder should have the same amplitude as the footwear hip, and the workwear shoulder should likewise match the make-up hip in voltage. This alignment creates what are known as the Pillars of Blythe, named after Sister Blythe of the Sacred Sisters of the Cloth. Sister Blythe noticed that the chronic spasms in her right shoulder improved when she took off her shoes, and disappeared after she had been barefoot for several days. Eventually she realized that her footwear hip had been more charged than the workwear shoulder, and plugging more footwear energy into her system with actual shoes was simply more than the shoulder could bear.

The sun room

Directly below the breastbone, from the solar plexus to the waist, is a zone which corresponds to the Phylonian market's change area. Known as the "sun room" by our ancestors, this internal zone has transformative potential just like the change area. Its capacity depends on one's internal space. Much can be said about the modern tendency to restrict this area, to belt it, squeeze it, somehow reduce its capacity. With our external focus during the last thousand years, this energetic ideal has strangely become a physical one, and millions of intelligent women stifle their change areas with control-top pantyhose and such things. It is too tragic for comment, although Lesley Letourneau has managed to find some hope in her book *The Unfettered Sun*. At the very least, understand that expanding this area takes considerable effort, given all the encouragement to make it smaller.

Phylo and you

Whatever was on the Phylonian woman's mind, her goal was to find just the right outfit, something that was both energizing and flattering. Choosing clothing these days is not so finely tuned an activity as it was, even for *ogoers*, so do begin your energy education by walking through the six departments at a modern women's wear store, alternating between stability (shoes, cosmetics, lingerie), and integration (workwear, sportswear, accessories) merchandise. Try to sense what attracts and repels you. To find out what your dominant energy type is, stand in the center of each department, turning slowly clockwise with your hand over your solar plexus. Notice any vibratory action. When you feel heat buzzing under your palm, you will know you are in your dominant energy field. If you feel prickly heat, or begin hyperventilating, you are overcharged with the particular energy of that department, and should balance yourself by going to an alternatively energized section of the store.

To prevent a chronically overcharged state, which can impair operations, *ogoers* should rebalance twice weekly. Predominantly a stability person, I am comforting to be around when I am balanced, but overstabilized, I tend to be on the bossy side. Shirley, in contrast, is an integrator, and on her good days is buoyant, chatty and highly social. At low periods she can be ingratiating, nosy and insincere. I balance myself by feeding ducks at the park, and Shirley regains equilibrium by leaning against the big beech tree outside the downtown library until she feels deeply rooted.

One should remember that we are primarily concerned with the energetics of an *ogoer*, rather than her physical shape. It takes a certain amount of mental retraining to keep thinking this way. Now, this doesn't mean that an *ogoer* just lets herself go, although don't let me stop you if the thought is appealing (and one should be entirely unrestrained from time to time, or moderation, as Phyllis put it between mouthfuls of chocolate bombé, has no terms of reference). The thing is, you mustn't forget what you are wearing while you experiment with your newfound circuitry. *Ogos* have a way of rebelling if they don't get the physical attention they're used to. Should tension develop between you and your *ogo* as you pursue your new interest in energy, refer to Harmonized purpose in Part I.

As an *ogoer* gains skill, the change zone in her solar plexus area expands into a large sphere where energy can freely move and transform. Eventually this sphere will energetically encompass the *ogoer*. While it grows, her stability and integration bridges converge. (Remember we are speaking about the energy body here— a short stability bridge does not correlate with physical compression in the shoulder region.) Bridge convergence means that the Pillars of Blythe also move toward each other, ultimately meeting at the spine to form a single column. Oppositional energies— workwear versus sportswear, feet versus face— unite in this column, balancing the *ogoer* between work and leisure, earth and sky. As D.T. Marshall explains in *Pythagoras Gets Dressed*, an *ogoer's* ideal energy body is perfectly symmetrical. It would look like this:

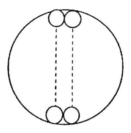

The ideal ogo energy body

Developing your energy body

Do not work at building up an energy body. It develops with awareness, not effort, and awareness will come with operational growth. You might like to practise a few balancing tricks while things develop, though, especially if you are prone to being overcharged by either stabilizing or integrating energies. If you are too stabilized and need more integration, spend twenty minutes twice a day with things that have a lot of interdependent components. Jigsaw puzzles, clocks and ant farms are examples. Tap your sternum regularly and pay special attention to your accessories. If you are overly integrated and need to stabilize, increase your intake of root vegetables, attend pottery and agricultural functions, and stand on a big rock for several minutes daily. Pat your stomach once in a while and sleep with your shoes beside your pillow.

Interconnections

Crossing wires

Once you have become familiar with your circuitry, you will feel the different frequencies of others. Most people and most events are imbalanced, being either too integrated or too stabilized. You will discover that certain groups of people have particular imbalances. Lawyers, for instance, tend to lean on their left legs. Group tendencies like this make it more efficient to do an energy reading of a room than of separate individuals, especially when one is entering an event.

Noy's model of group dynamics

Every group has energy fluctuations. On a practical level, the trick is to jump in and out of conversations at the right moments; going with the flow, so to speak. Many *ogoers* rely on Tammy Noy's surge and retreat model of group behaviour. Coining the term "force of total integrative power"— or *f-tip*— Noy understood that a group can harness the total power of its members, regardless of how potent or impotent individuals may feel. (An excellent example would be the skirmish at the Living with Lassitude conference, where participants demanded more muffins.) After several weeks of *f-tip* charting, Noy also discovered that *f-tips* rise and fall in waveforms throughout the day, occasionally surging into something big. I have experienced only two *f-tip* surges, the most recent being at the Small Appliance convention, when someone began to sob and we all joined in, including the keynote speaker, who became so distraught she knocked over a blender.

If not for the force of aggregate stability energies (*f-ase*) which usually keep things under control, we would always be crying, or revolting. *F-ases* are the millions of separate undercurrents that collectively exert a strong downward pull. I find the Noy grid helpful in visualizing the *f-ase* / *f-tip* interaction: as you can see they alternate; *f-ases* exert maximum pull at the height of an *f-tip* wave, then relax, or lift, during an *f-tip* lull.

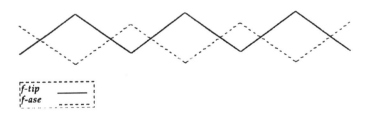

f-tip ⎯⎯⎯
f-ase - - - - - - -

Noy's Matrix

The *f-ase* rhythm can become irregular, since it is determined by individual pulses, while *f-tips* are more or less steady. When agitated or relaxed, *f-ases* can get out of sync, even to the point of swelling an *f-tip* surge rather than holding it back. Called peak convergence, such a moment can have explosive power, as in the Starkish revolt, or it can be intensely cathartic, as in the Small Appliance incident.

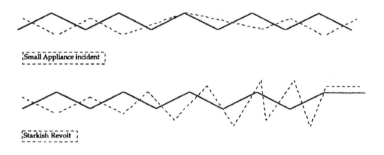

Small Appliance incident

Starkish Revolt

P-zone

After Noy's death, her good friend Lily Sander developed an addendum to the surge and retreat model, identifying the blank space between *f-tip* and *f-ase* lines, and naming it the zone of potentiality, or *p-zone*. As you may have guessed, an event's *p-zone* is where *ogoers* are uniquely adept and everyone else is not. It is the place between this and that, coming and going, starting and finishing, where we must all bob around waiting for the next current. Always the girl for food metaphors, Trina J. calls *p-zone* the marination station. I think of it simply as The Pause.

Performing in the p-zone

You will know a *p-zone* moment by the slight rise in humidity and decreased air flow, even when fans or air conditioners are operating, and the uneasiness these changes cause. There may be an increase in twitchiness, hiccups, and facial contractions among those present. Never rush during a *p-zone*, or gesture in an extravagant fashion. Speak in as low a register as you can and touch people's hands. The uncertainty of a *p-zone* means that people are primed for reassurance. Perhaps you recall the landscaping convention in 1997. After a morning of workshops on perennials, where participants almost caused an f-tip surge with their zealous exchanges of expertise, and following the keynote address on shaded rock gardens, the hall became still and quiet. My effusive tablemate, Donna deSilva, closed her garden photo album and whispered, "Perhaps my Astilbe requires more acidic soil." My role was clear: I gently re-opened her album, found the photos of her Ostrich Plum Astilbe and assured her that it was magnificent. *Ogoers* throughout the room were similiarly engaged, and by the time the p-zone passed, we were deeply appreciated and indispensable. Use the reassurance skills you learned in Part II while remaining sensitive to energy fluctuations. You may be required to provide meta or micro reassurance, depending on the vibratory quality of the p-zone. When p-zone currents are undulating rapidly, people need to hear meta messages, for instance, that anything is possible and any second now their lives may be transformed. Micro-assurance addresses concrete, immediate concerns, as in the landscaping convention. If you feel strong but shallow currents, your tablemates may simply need confirmation that Dr. Lache from Duke University is indeed the next speaker.

Group longings

We mustn't think that because we understand *f-ases* and *f-tips* we are immune to their power. The few times I have succumbed to volunteer activity I am quite sure I have been affected by an *f-ase* pull, which makes people want badly to be part of something. I am thinking of a meeting I came across and was pulled into, despite other plans for the day. A small group was planning a baseball tournament as a goodbye party for their beloved colleague. Certainly I was curious about this co-worker, and perhaps I am sentimental about baseball, but mostly it was the integrative power of the group that pulled me, inexorably, towards them. And so I spent a not unpleasant day skewering hotdogs. As it turned out, the colleague, Susanna, was splendid, and the cousin of Maureen Crighton, a talented *ogoer* in Lethbridge.

The desire to belong is one of those things that one learns

to live with. When you feel the craving, try to find a two or three day event you can immerse yourself in. Last year's International Square Dancing Round-up was a godsend for me last spring.

The long pause

After a while you will notice that longing becomes most acute when you are deeply involved in a group. (Deep involvement means that you are highly sensitized and responsive to group energies, not that you are necessarily listening to anyone.) Because *p-zones* are so subtle, yet so potent— remember, the *p* stands for potential— they require an *ogoer's* deepest involvement and create her most intense longing. One has a heightened sense of being both connected and separate. In sad moments, when the potential of The Pause feels more empty than inspiring, summon the spirits of your *ogoer* ancestors to keep you company. If no one comes, concentrate on the historical links of your *ogo*. Imagine it as a loincloth, an Assyrian sarong, an Egyptian *schenti*, a Greek *chiton*, and so forth. Some *ogoers* have actually felt the fabric of their *ogo* change from leather to wool to linen as they did this, but even if this doesn't occur for you, cherish the timelessness of your *ogo*.

Inevitably, an *f-tip* will sweep over The Pause and longing will disappear as integrative energy takes over. If an *ogoer* was having difficulty with longing during The Pause she may be too eager to be integrative, and when the *f-tip* crests, she may forget herself entirely. Who knows what momentous events happened because an *ogoer* forgot she was *ogoing*? Although Anita Jamn's *99 Forgetful* Ogoers, *121 Memorable Moments in World History* will not be released until spring, I understand that it includes the Magna Carta, the Treaty of Versailles, and Belgium's Bill C-93.

On an unremarkable level, I had a forgetful moment several weeks ago during a period of terrible longing. At the Meadow-lane Condominium Annual Breakfast Meeting, an *f-tip* surge occurred during by-law negotiations, and before I knew it I had made a motion to amend the pet policy. (As it stood, the policy allowed for a maximum of three pets per home, which was clearly excessive, given the desecration of flower beds by cats and the earsplitting barking, described by Mrs. Schlicken, that occurred whenever a fire truck or ambulance wailed by. I put forth a motion to amend the policy so new residents could only have one pet, with a grandfather clause so current residents could keep, but not replace, their current pets. It was passed unanimously.) Throughout the room, heads leaned toward each other and whispered, *Who is that?* Fortunately, everyone was too tired to care, and I was able to stay for lunch.

Acknowledgements

This book is largely the result of Greg Hollinghead's teaching and guidance. I am very grateful to him.

The thoughts, impressions, and idiosyncracies of other teachers, friends and family are woven through *One Good Outfit*. For your help and enthusiasm, in all its various forms, heartfelt thanks to Dan Aire, Lisa Austin, Les Bergen, Diane Brown, Garnet Brown, Kathy Brown, Maureen Brown, Jennifer Chambers, Patty Dusel, Donna Gruhlke, Michele Kelly, Mary Macnamee, Edwina Madill, Gaylord Madill, Maureen Malloy, Alison Mustard, Francine Ricard, Sandra Sammartino, Eunice Scarfe, Michelle Stack, Yvette Stack, Denise Thompson, Kerry Thompson, Karen White.